HOBBY HANDBOOKS™

ROCKS & FOSSILS

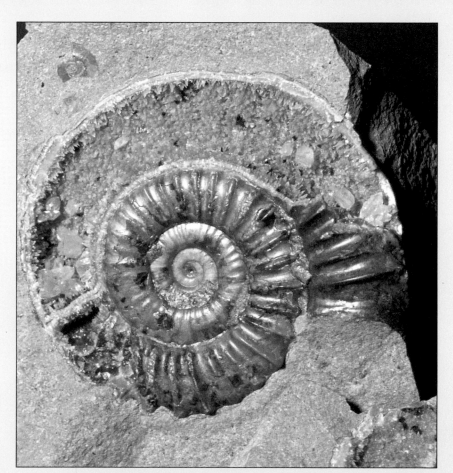

RAY OLIVER

RANDOM HOUSE 🏠 NEW YORK

ACKNOWLEDGMENTS

Many of the photographs in this book were specially taken for Reed Children's Books by David Johnson. The publisher would like to thank the author, and Dr Robert Symes and Mr Alan Hart of the Department of Mineralogy at the Natural History Museum, Exhibition Road, London SW7, for their invaluable assistance in supplying the equipment and specimens for photography; and the following individuals and organizations for providing the photographs used in this book:
Ancient Art and Architecture Collection 44 bottom left, /B. Norman 32 (bottom), Ardea London Ltd 57 top. Bridgeman Art Library 47 top left, /John Bethell 22 top, Paul Brierley 59 bottom right, Bruce Coleman Ltd, /Alfred Pasicka 59 top left, /Fritz Prenzel 71 center left, /Michel Viard 44 bottom center, Collections, /Brian Shuel 46 left. Geoscience Features Picture Library 17 center, 19 top right, 21 bottom, 22 bottom right, 39 bottom, 47 top right, 50 center, 50 bottom left, 50 bottom center, 50 bottom right, 51 top left, 51 top center, 51 top right, 51 bottom left, 51 bottom right, 52 bottom, 59 top right, 67 bottom left, 67 bottom center, 67 bottom right, 68 top, 69 top, 73 top. Michael Holford 28 bottom. Imagine 29 bottom left, 29 bottom right. Images Colour Library 58 left, 71 top. Frank Lane Picture Agency 16 top, /A.R. Hamblin 66 left, /Steve McCutcheon 25 bottom right, /M. Nimmo 29 top, /Peter Reynolds 20 center, /Walter Robdich 48 top left, © Arthur Montes De Oca 20 top. Natural History Museum, London 55 top, 56 left, 56-57 center, 56-57 bottom, 57 bottom right, 70-71, 71 center right, Reed International Books Ltd/David Johnson 8 top, 10-11, 12-13, 12 bottom left, 14-15, 16 left, 17 right, 18-19, 21 left, 22-23, 26-27, 30-31 bottom, 32-33, 32 bottom, 34-35, 37 right, 38 bottom, 40-41, 46-47, 60,61, 65, 66 right, 68 center, 69 bottom, 72-73, 74 bottom. Rida Photo Library / David Bayliss 22 bottom left, 38 top, 52 top left. RTZ Ltd 49 top left. Science Photo Library /Roberto de Gugliemo 62 left, /Manfred Kage 67 center right, /J. Koivula 50 top, /Martin Land 19 top left, 52 top right, /Andrew McClenaghan 36 bottom, /Claude Nuridsany & Maric Perennou 67 top, /Philippe Plailly 64 left, /David Parker 53 bottom left, 64 right, 75 right, /Dr Morley Read 48 top right, /Sinclair Stammers 8 bottom, 51 center right, 51 bottom right, 75 left, /David Taylor 36 bottom left. Sotheby's 68 bottom center, 68 bottom right. © Sinclair Stammers 64 bottom. By courtesy of the Board of Trustees of the Victoria & Albert Museum /D.P.P. Naish 71 bottom right, Tony Waltham Geoslides 42 top, 43 bottom. © John S. Whiteley 44-45.

Illustrators:
David Ashby (Garden Studio): 11, 12, 13 (left), 15, 17 (right), 20, 24 (right), 34, 35, 37, 41, 42, 43, 48, 49, 53, 60-61 (top), 61 (right), 62-63. Peter Bull Art: 9, 16-17 (center), 19, 21, 23, 24 (left), 25, 30-31, 33, 44, 45, 54, 55, 59-59, 60 (left), 60-61 (bottom), 69.

Editor: Andrew Farrow
Designers: Anne Sharples, Mark Summersby
Series Designer: Anne Sharples
Production Controller: Linda Spillane
Picture Researcher: Caroline Hensman

First American edition, 1993

Library of Congress Cataloging in Publication Data
Oliver, Ray.
Rocks & fossils / Ray Oliver. — 1st American ed.
p.   cm. — (Hobby handbooks)
Includes index.
1. Rocks—Collection and preservation—Juvenile literature.
2. Fossils—Collection and preservation—Juvenile literature.
[1. Rocks—Collectors and collecting. 2. Fossils—Collection and preservation.]
I. Title.   II. Title: Rocks and fossils.   III. Series.
QE433.6.045 1993
552'.0075—dc20   92–44791

ISBN 0-679-82661-0   ISBN 0-679-92661-5 (lib. bdg.)

Manufactured in Great Britain

1 2 3 4 5 6 7 8 9 10

CONTENTS

MINERALS, ROCKS, AND FOSSILS

Collecting minerals, rocks, and fossils is a great way to learn about the natural world. It is one of the few areas of science where amateurs still make important discoveries. If you study rocks and fossils you will be finding out about the materials from which the Earth is made, and also about the history of the Earth.

WHAT'S THE DIFFERENCE?

Minerals are naturally occurring, nonliving substances, such as quartz or diamond. Each mineral is made of many particles. In most minerals, these particles are arranged in a regular order, forming crystals. Substances such as sugar form crystals, but they are plant- or animal-based, so they are not minerals.

Quartz is a common mineral in the Earth's crust. Quartz is found in several forms — as sand on the beach, as gemstones such as purple amethyst, and also as bands of flint in chalk.

ROCKS

Rocks are made of minerals, just as walls are made of bricks. Some rocks contain only one mineral, all the "bricks" being the same. Chalk is like this. The only mineral present is called calcium carbonate. However, most rocks are mixtures of two or more different minerals. For example, granite contains the three minerals quartz, mica, and feldspar.

Rocks form very slowly, often over millions of years. An exception is the rock that is formed by an erupting volcano. Huge amounts of liquid volcanic rock, called lava, can be released in just hours or days.

WHAT ABOUT FOSSILS?

Fossils are the remains or marks of things that were alive thousands or millions of years ago. Sometimes fossils still consist of their original material, such as sharks' teeth or shells. Usually the remains have been fossilized, or chemically changed. This means that the original bones or leaves have been replaced by minerals such as quartz. Sometimes only an impression of the creature's shape is left in the rocks; this is called a fossil print or cast. The preserved footprints of dinosaurs are regarded as fossils.

Granite is a rock made of three different minerals. The glassy mineral is quartz, the black specks are mica, and the largest crystals are feldspar.

granite

quartz

mica

feldspar

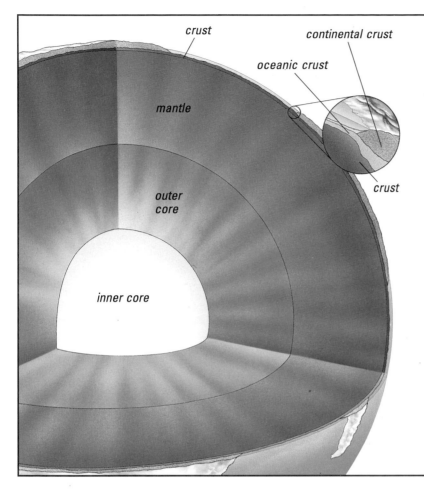

crust

continental crust

oceanic crust

mantle

outer core

crust

inner core

UNDER THE SURFACE

Nobody is certain what the structure of the Earth is like. The best evidence suggests that the interior is made of different layers of material. In the center is the inner core. Around this is the outer core. Both parts of the Earth's core probably consist of metals such as iron and nickel. The next thick region is the mantle, which stretches up to the crust. The crust occurs as two types of material. The sea floors are made of heavy, dense rocks, such as basalt. Above these are the continents. The continental crust is less dense and is made of sections called plates. These plates are moving continually but slowly, less than an inch per year.

Although the inner core of the Earth is very hot — up to 13,000°F — the great pressure of the surrounding material keeps it solid. The rocks melt only when the great pressure is relieved. Then the magma, or molten rock, tries to rise to the surface, following cracks in the rock. As the magma reaches the surface it cools, and minerals "freeze" solid to form crystals. Eventually the rock solidifies.

This is a collection of beautifully preserved ammonites (left). Ammonites were mollusks, related to nautiluses and squids, that lived beneath the sea between 65 and 400 million years ago. Ammonite fossils are common in marine rocks.

COLLECTING ROCKS AND FOSSILS

Rock and fossil collecting is a fascinating hobby. You can go hunting for specimens, carry out experiments, and learn how rocks, minerals, and fossils are formed. It's a good idea to join a club or society, because the other members will share your enthusiasm and help you learn more about your hobby. In many towns and cities there are natural history or archaeological societies, often with a junior section. At a club you may find out about mail-order dealers, rock shops, or good places to look for specimens. There may also be field trips to interesting sites.

READ ALL ABOUT IT

This book is all about collecting and studying rocks and fossils. First you'll find out about equipment and how to use it. Then there are sections on types of rocks and how to find them. This book also tells you about the many fascinating properties of minerals and how to test and identify them, and it looks in detail at mineral waters, mining, and metals. There are sections on fossils and dinosaurs, on the hundreds of crystals that can be found all around us, and on the fabulous world of gemstones and jewelry. Finally, the book shows you how to display your collection and suggests ways in which you can develop your hobby. Whether you want to hunt for specimens, or just like to read about them, we hope that you find this book useful. The most important thing is that you enjoy yourself. If you find a rare specimen, you may even become famous as well!

EQUIPMENT

You can start collecting rocks and fossils with nothing more complicated than a plastic pail or bag to hold any specimens that you find. The serious collector will need more equipment than this, though you may already have many items around your home.

HAMMER
Every serious collector will need a strong hammer. A geological hammer has a square end for striking rocks and a pickax end to pry out specimens.
There's no need to buy a huge hammer — get one that's not too heavy for you to hold properly.

MAP AND COMPASS
A large-scale map of the area will help you find your way and allow you to record the best locations for future trips. A compass will not only give you directions but can be used to detect magnetic minerals, too.

CHISEL AND BRUSH
A strong masonry chisel is useful to split apart rock layers, in which fossils may be found. Some rocks split more easily in one direction, like wood chopped along the grain. Other rocks are so soft that you can use a soft brush or an old toothbrush to clean around fossils.

SAFETY FIRST!
When you see this symbol on one of the following pages, ask an adult to help you with the experiment or activity described. Always wear safety glasses and protective gloves when using acid or a naked flame, or when chipping rock.

CHIPPING AND HAMMERING

If you can't remove a sample by scraping with a chisel or spike, you'll need to use a hammer. Use only as much force as necessary to split the rock or you will damage the sample. You may need to support the rock you are hammering so that it doesn't fall away — and be careful not to hit your hand! **Always wear safety glasses when hammering** so that chips don't get into your eyes.

Always hammer gently at first when trying to separate a specimen from rock. If possible, chip away from the specimen, so that you won't damage it if your chisel slips. A fossil will have formed slowly over millions of years. Take your time so that you don't make mistakes.

Carefully trim unwanted material from the **edges** of the sample before packing it up to take home. Leave any final chipping or trimming until you get home. One blow that is too hard can split the whole sample.

NOTEBOOK AND PENCIL

Once you have a sample you will need to describe it and note where it was found. Take a notebook and pencil to record your finds, because it is very easy to forget important details at the end of a long day in the field.

STURDY CLOTHES

Safety glasses or goggles are essential to protect your eyes from rock splinters. A hard hat is necessary if you are working near a cliff face; quarry owners will insist that you wear a safety hat before granting permission to visit. Always wear warm clothes and a sturdy pair of shoes or boots.

SIEVING

Nests of sieves are used for sorting loose material into grains of different sizes. Put the nest of sieves together and add a scoop of the crushed mixture to the top sieve.

Shake the nest gently to separate the mixture according to the size of the particles. The different size meshes in the sieves will hold back particles that are too large to go through their holes.

Remove each sieve and tip its contents onto some newspaper so you can examine them with a hand lens. You may need to crush large pieces and sieve them again.

BAGS AND CONTAINERS

The easiest way to wrap specimens safely is to use sheets of newspaper, remembering to include a label with each sample. The bag that you use to carry the samples will need to be strong because of their weight. Canvas bags, of the type that you can buy in army surplus stores, are ideal. Plastic containers, such as empty margarine tubs, can be used to hold sands and other smaller specimens that won't break easily. Don't use glass containers, which you might break while you are scrambling around.

⊗ ROCK AND FOSSIL PROJECTS

Many rock and fossil enthusiasts join clubs, take field trips, and look for other ways to learn more about their hobby. Page 74 suggests fossil projects; page 75 lists addresses of museums and geological organizations to contact for more information.

SIEVES AND TROWEL

Clay or sand can be sifted with a kitchen flour sieve to remove small fossils for examination. You can buy a nest of sieves in which each sieve has progressively smaller mesh holes. Different sizes of material collect in each sieve and can be examined separately. A trowel is particularly useful for digging in gravel and loose rock.

WRAPPING SAMPLES

Place the specimen near one corner of a sheet of newspaper. Make sure the delicate side is facing up.

Next, carefully fold the sides of the newspaper over the specimen.

Roll up the specimen in the newspaper, keeping the whole package neatly and firmly together.

The rolled package will have most of the folded newspaper protecting the delicate part of the specimen.

FIELD SKETCHES

You will not be able to take away some of the samples you find. To keep a record of these, make a field sketch using a pencil and graph paper. Draw the sample from more than one angle and put a scale on your drawings. Include every detail that could help you identify the sample later, such as color and texture. When you get home compare your sketch to reference books. Or you could make a sketch map of your local area, marking on it the types of building stones you can find.

Ammonite replaced by calcite.
Found partly embedded in limestone.
July 27, 1992.
Crow cliffs.

2 in

WORKING AT HOME

Some of the most interesting work on rocks, minerals, and fossils can be carried out at home. For example, you may want to identify a mineral sample by testing its properties, or separate a fossil completely from its surrounding rock. For these investigations, and others described in this book, some more specialized equipment is needed. Do not use equipment that will later be used to prepare food.

C-CLAMP
A C-clamp (right) is useful for holding samples firmly in place while you trim them. Always prepare a good working area for testing and working on specimens.

MEASURING EQUIPMENT
A balance or scale is needed to measure the weight of your samples for density tests (p. 35). An ordinary kitchen scale will be accurate enough for large specimens. Use a small measuring cup or a plastic cylinder (shown at right) with a scale to find the volume of a sample.

MAGNIFYING GLASS
If you have a magnifying glass or a binocular microscope, you will be able to examine the fine details of your specimens. A pocket hand lens is useful for studying specimens in the field.

ACID

Weak acid is used for removing rock (right) and conducting fizz tests (p. 34). The most suitable acid is acetic acid in vinegar. **Only carry out these tests in the presence of an adult. Acids are corrosive, so always wear safety glasses and rubber gloves.**

REMOVING ROCK

Acids can be used to dissolve limestone (calcium carbonate) rocks to release fossils found in them. Protect each fossil with a layer of clear nail polish because some fossils, too, will dissolve in acid.

Carefully paint the exposed parts of the fossil with clear nail polish. Wait until the polish hardens.

Place the sample in vinegar and leave it in a safe and well-ventilated place for a day. Do not seal the container.

Using protective gloves and safety glasses, carefully rinse the vinegar from the sample using lots of running water. If necessary, repeat all these steps until the fossil is free of the rock.

BOOKS

Books are essential for identifying specimens. A well-illustrated field guide will describe and show many types of rocks, minerals, and fossils. Local guide books may also have some useful information about interesting geological features in the area.

15

IGNEOUS ROCKS

There are three types of rock in the Earth's crust: igneous, sedimentary, and metamorphic rocks. The first to form were the igneous, or primary, rocks. Igneous rocks are formed at high temperatures. They are still forming today, one example being the lava that flows from a volcano.

Igneous rocks can be recognized by their crystals. Glassy obsidian has few, tiny crystals, basalt contains very fine crystals, and gabbro has large crystals.

basalt

obsidian

gabbro

A volcano (above) can be like a bottle of soda. When the pressure on the lava is released, gas bubbles dissolved in it expand. They rise to the surface, driving the lava out of the volcano.

TYPES OF IGNEOUS ROCK

When lava escapes from a volcano it loses its heat quickly and solidifies. There isn't much time for any crystals to grow in the cooling lava flow. You can recognize lavas because they often look glassy with few, if any, obvious crystals. The crystals are there but they are very small. Sometimes the lava will have lots of holes in it where gases bubbled out of the molten rock. One of the most common lavas cools to form the rock basalt, which is often black. You may need to use a hand lens to find any crystals in basalt.

Not all igneous rocks escape at the Earth's surface like lavas. Most igneous rocks are formed deep underground, where the rocks above trap the heat like a blanket. Rocks that cool underground take a long time to solidify. This means that these sorts of igneous rocks have larger crystals than volcanic rocks. The best known example is granite, a very hard rock. Although it is formed underground, granite can be seen at the Earth's surface because the rocks above have been worn away over million of years.

When magma is very hot and under pressure, it forces its way to the surface. If there is a weak spot in the crust, the magma escapes and a volcano forms (left). Some lavas can spread for miles, causing great destruction (below right).

LAVA FLOWS

Different types of lava flow downhill away from a volcano at different speeds. Some lavas are viscous, or thick, and flow slowly. Being quite thick, they sometimes block the escape of gas from the volcano, causing a buildup of gas. When the pressure gets very great, the volcano erupts violently. Other lavas are very hot and runny and will flow a long way. They usually cool to form basalt.

Pumice (above) is formed in volcanic eruptions. It is often light enough to float on water.

ROCK HOUND'S HINT
Many igneous rocks are very hard and can be polished to an attractive finish. Look for their use in buildings and monuments.

OTHER IGNEOUS ROCKS

Granites are light-colored rocks, because they contain pale-colored feldspar crystals. Some igneous rocks are much darker than granite. One example is gabbro, which is also much heavier than a similarly sized piece of granite — gabbro is more dense than granite.

You may have a piece of igneous rock in your bathroom, for scraping away dirt. It is pale colored, very light for its size, and full of bubbles. It may even float in water. This rock is called pumice and is formed by some types of volcano.

LAVA FLOWS

Add separate pools of different liquids along one edge of a metal baking tray. Try cooking oil, molasses, and maple syrup as your examples of lava. Slowly raise the edge of the tray to start the liquids flowing down the slope. You can measure the angle of the slope using a protractor.

Which is the most viscous liquid? It will be the most sticky one, the one that flows most slowly down the slope. You can also investigate the effect of temperature on lava flows. Cool the liquids in a fridge and then try them again to see if there is a difference in speed of flow.

SEDIMENTARY ROCKS

When rocks are worn away by the weather, they break down into smaller pieces of rocks and minerals, forming sediment. Sediments harden into sedimentary rocks — rocks made of pieces of other rocks. They contain grains of material held together by different kinds of natural cement. The grains often show bands or patterns running through them. Some sedimentary rocks are made of shells of sea creatures or even of salt layers.

sandstone

chalk

SANDSTONES

Sandstones are usually easy to recognize. They look as though beach sand has been glued together. Sandstones are often used in buildings. If you look closely with a hand lens, you might see the shape of individual grains. Sandstones formed from desert sands have worn edges because the grains bumped together. Some sandstones formed in the sea have ripple marks in them, just like the marks of water ripples you can see on a beach.

conglomerate

algal limestone

STRATA

As rocks wear away, the pieces are carried by wind or water until they settle. Often the material reaches the sea where it settles in layers on the sea bed. Large and heavy pieces settle quickly. Tiny pieces of sand or fine mud settle more slowly on the seabed — they often travel many miles before settling. New layers, or strata, of sedimentary rock slowly form. Even under the weight of new layers above, it can take millions of years before the soft sand or mud turns into a hard sandstone or mudstone.

Can you guess what to look for when trying to identify a rock as being a sedimentary rock? One obvious clue is the presence of layers. Another strong clue is the presence of fossils in the rock. The shells of sea creatures fall to the seabed when they die, and can be preserved as fossils in the newly forming sedimentary rocks, such as limestone.

mudstone

breccia

Sedimentary rocks form in similar ways, but they can look very different. In chalk the particles are so small that you can hardly see them. In a conglomerate the rounded pebbles can be very big.

limestone

Strata are layers of sedimentary rock. Most rock strata are horizontal when they are formed, as in the sandstone pictured above. However, violent earth movements can crush and bend rock strata into amazing patterns (left).

CHALK

Chalk is another common sedimentary rock. There is no other rock that looks so white. Chalk is a very pure form of limestone. Limestones come in several colors, yellow-white and gray being the most common. You may find lumps of the mineral flint, a much harder gray material, in chalk.

Other sedimentary rocks include mudstones and clays, which consist of fine particles. There are also rocks called conglomerates, made up of pebbles.

clay

COMPACTION AND CEMENTATION

As sediments settle on the seabed, their weight presses down on the layers below. This presses out water from the material and compacts, or squeezes, the particles together, forming sedimentary rock. There are several natural cements, such as silica in sandstones, and calcium carbonate in limestones, that stick particles together to make new rocks. The cement is left as a coating on the particles when water is squeezed out.

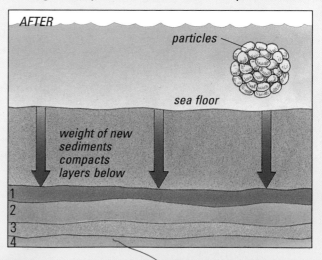

SALT DEPOSITS

Salt flats are a special type of sedimentary rock. They are formed when salt lakes and seas dry up, leaving shiny masses of crystals behind. This is what is happening at the moment in the Dead Sea in Israel. All over the world there are salt flats and lakes, as well as layers of salt underground. Salt flats provide ideal surfaces for attempts to break the land speed record.

Salt is called an evaporite deposit since it is left behind when water evaporates. You can carry out an experiment to make your own salt deposit. Start by making up a very strong solution of salt by dissolving as much as you can in some water. Pour the salty water into a shallow tray of sand until all the sand is covered. Leave the water in a warm place to evaporate. When the sand has dried out, examine the salt layer. You may be able to see little cubes of salt—salt crystals. Look for patterns of cracks in the surface of the salt. These will probably look like the cracks you can find in real rocks. If you find salt crystals in a rock, it shows that the weather was very dry when that rock was formed long ago.

When water evaporates from a sea faster than it is replaced, the water dries up to leave salt flats (above). These are good places to speed test cars. Mud cracks form when mud dries out, and can be preserved as rocks (right) that show the original pattern of cracks.

RIPPLES ON THE BEACH

Use a large shallow tray for this experiment. Add a layer of sand about ½ in. deep and then pour in enough water to cover the sand to a depth of 1 in. When the sand has settled again, move a ruler up and down to make a pattern of waves in the water. Look at the patterns that form in the sand and make a sketch. Try moving the ruler at different speeds to see if the pattern changes. You can find ripple marks just like these in sedimentary rocks, sometimes with preserved footprints as well.

STRATA IN A JAR

Use this simple experiment to see how sedimentary rock layers are formed. For best results use different colors of mud, sand, and pebbles, as well as different sizes. Half fill a tall glass jar with water, and add mud, sand, and pebbles. Stir the mixture very well and then leave it to settle. Although some materials will sink quickly, you may find that others will take several hours to settle. Eventually the materials separate to form layers. Where are the largest pieces? Make a careful note of what you find, as well as a sketch. You may find a similar pattern of layers in real rocks, as in the cliff in the photo or the diagram on the right.

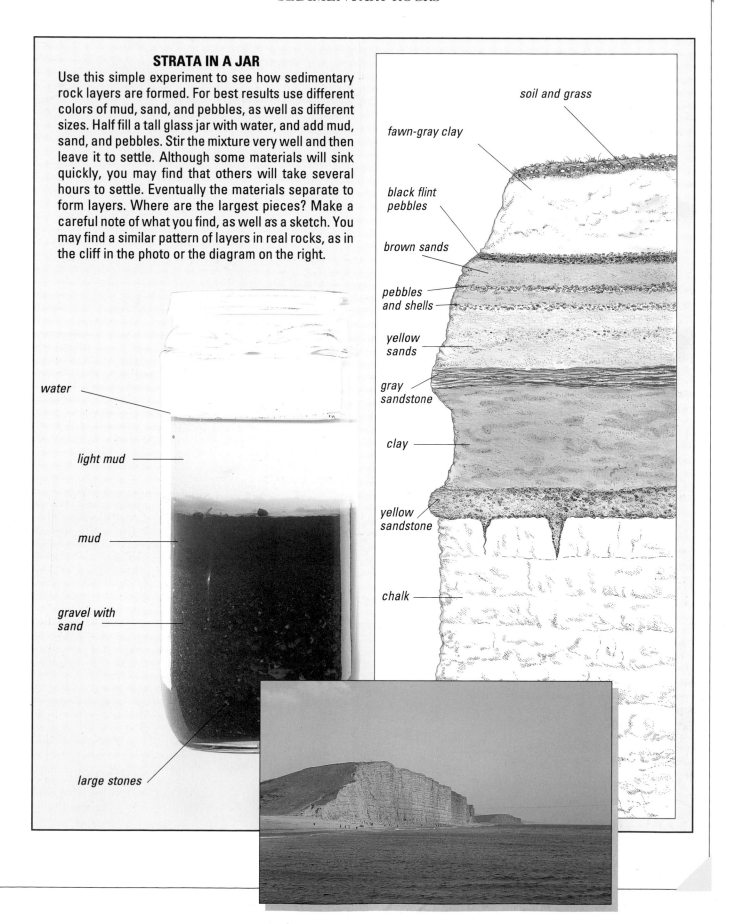

water

light mud

mud

gravel with sand

large stones

soil and grass

fawn-gray clay

black flint pebbles

brown sands

pebbles and shells

yellow sands

gray sandstone

clay

yellow sandstone

chalk

METAMORPHIC ROCKS

SOME METAMORPHIC ROCKS

Metamorphic rock	Original rock	Cause
marble	limestone	heat
slate	mudstone and shale	pressure
schist	mudstone and shale	heat and pressure
gneiss	mudstone and shale	heat and pressure
metaquartzite	sandstone	heat

marble

All metamorphic rocks have been changed from other kinds of rock. The changes are usually caused by great heat within the Earth, or pressure from movements in the crust, or by both together. Just as soft clay can be fired in a kiln to form hard, brittle pottery, so rocks can be changed by metamorphism. You are unlikely to find fossils in metamorphic rocks because heat and pressure will have destroyed them.

SLATE
Slate, which is formed under great pressure under the Earth's surface, is one of the easiest metamorphic rocks to recognize. The great pressure pushes on all the minerals inside the slate until they point in the same direction. This means that slate can be split into thin sheets, and for many years has been used for roofing.

When slate is split for roofing, much of the rock is broken and wasted. If you go to a slate quarry there will be plenty of samples for you to examine. Slate can be gray, green, or even purple.

SCHIST
If the pressure and heat are very great, the rock can change into a glittering new metamorphic rock called schist. This rock is usually bent into wavy layers, often containing shiny, black mica crystals.

Sometimes you can find gemstones called garnets in schist. They are usually red and have been formed by changes to the original rock. These garnets are in mica schist.

Slates for roofing (below) are made by quarrying blocks of slate and then splitting them along the weakest planes in the rock. The best slate splits easily into flat sheets when a chisel is applied in the right place. The sheets can then be trimmed to the right size.

22

slate   *schist*   *gneiss*   *metaquartzite*

The Earth's rocks are naturally recycled over millions of years (right). Igneous rocks are broken down by weathering to form sedimentary rocks. These in turn can be changed into metamorphic rocks. Marble (left and below right) has been used for many years to decorate magnificent rooms and buildings.

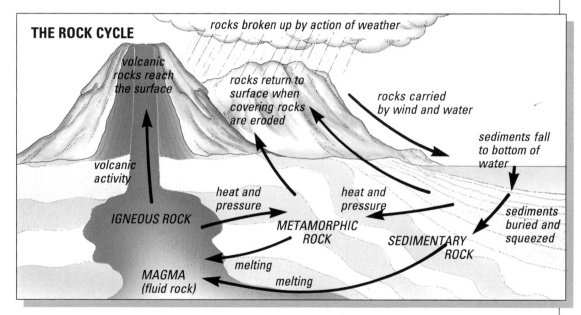

THE ROCK CYCLE

rocks broken up by action of weather

volcanic rocks reach the surface

rocks return to surface when covering rocks are eroded

rocks carried by wind and water

volcanic activity

sediments fall to bottom of water

heat and pressure

heat and pressure

IGNEOUS ROCK

METAMORPHIC ROCK

SEDIMENTARY ROCK

sediments buried and squeezed

melting

MAGMA (fluid rock)

melting

MARBLE

This is the best-known metamorphic rock of all. When limestones are heated and squeezed by metamorphic changes underground the result is marble. If the original limestone was very pure, the marble will be white, hard, and have a sugary texture. Impurities in the limestone will produce beautiful colors and bands in the marble. Marble does not split easily and must be mined very precisely in order to avoid damage to it. However, it can be carved and polished and so has been a favorite material for sculptors for thousands of years. It is also broken into slabs and used for tiles and for decorating buildings.

MOVEMENTS IN THE EARTH

The surface of the Earth is changing all the time because of the movement of the crust. Also, the rocks of the Earth's crust are continually being built up, worn away, and re-formed. These changes are usually very slow. Except for volcanic eruptions and earthquakes, most geological changes take much longer than one human lifetime.

MOUNTAINS

Mountains are the most prominent rock features of the Earth's crust. There are four main types of mountain—volcanic, dome, block, and fold. Volcanic mountains are built up as volcanoes, as molten igneous rock is forced up through a weak point in the crust. Many islands are the tops of underwater volcanoes. Dome mountains are formed as pressure builds up beneath the surface, forcing the earth up to form huge mounds.

FOLDS
Movements of the Earth's crust can make the original horizontal layers buckle into folds. Anticlines are upward folds, synclines sag down (p. 31).

faulted fold

FOLD MOUNTAINS

For this experiment, roll out some rectangular layers of clay of different colors. Put the layers on top of each other on a smooth surface. Each layer of clay represents a rock stratum.

Next, hold opposite ends of the clay layers and push them toward each other. Note what happens as the mountain grows. As you push, stress is put on the layers and they may even split apart. You can try similar experiments with piles of blankets or even layers of gelatin.

Sometimes, movement of the crust forces huge blocks of the crust to rise up and others to sink. This is how block mountains are formed. Block mountains often have flat tops, with flat-bottomed valleys between them. Fold mountains have curved layers of rock. Try the experiment above and you will find out how scientists believe fold mountains are formed.

When the Earth's crust moves, huge forces push against the rocks. Under this great strain, the rocks try to move. Sometimes they bend or flow, producing folds (left), but sometimes they break, forming a fault (right). Try the experiments on these pages to show both types of rock movement.

EARTHQUAKE!

Start by supporting the ends of a stick on some blocks so that the stick looks like a bridge. Now hang some weights from the center of the stick. Keep adding weights until the stick breaks. Sometimes real rocks behave like this underground — they don't flow or bend like clay, but resist the strain until they break. When this happens there is an earthquake.

FAULTS

These are some of the types of faults that occur when rocks break.

NORMAL FAULT

fault plane

upthrown block

downthrown block

REVERSE FAULT

THRUST FAULT

TEAR FAULT

Earthquakes usually happen without warning and last only a few seconds or minutes. The amount of energy released in an earthquake can be large enough to wreck buildings, destroy bridges, and move roads. Modern buildings can be designed to withstand most earthquakes.

FINDING ROCKS

A QUICK GUIDE TO ROCKS

This is a key to the guide on the next page. It shows how geologists define the different sizes of rock grains.

Grain Size		
Size (in)		**Name**
Less than 0.00015		Clay
0.00015 -	0.0025	Silt
0.0025 -	0.079	Sand
0.079 -	0.16	Gravel
0.16 -	2.5	Pebbles
And		
0.0025 -	0.005	Very Fine
0.005 -	0.01	Fine
0.01 -	0.02	Medium
0.02 -	0.04	Coarse
0.04 -	0.08	Very Coarse

KEY
I = Igneous
M = Metamorphic
S = Sedimentary

Before you start hunting for rocks and minerals, you need to know what to look for and where to go. Probably the best place to start looking for information about the presence of rocks and fossils in your area is your school or local town library. Don't forget to look in the telephone book, which will have the addresses of local geological and industrial museums.

BUILDING A REFERENCE LIBRARY

It's not difficult to build up a good reference library you can use in your studies. Besides buying new books, ask for them as birthday presents, or look in secondhand bookshops. Local newspapers often run stories about finds made in the area, perhaps when the foundations of a new building or road are being dug. Cut these out and stick them in a scrapbook, along with any magazine articles that you find.

Tell friends about your hobby, and perhaps they will collect information for you. You could even take photographs of interesting rocks or buildings and add these to your scrapbook. It won't be long before you have a unique and valuable record to show other friends who share your hobby.

PHOTOGRAPHY

Photos can be an invaluable record of where you have found specimens. Take a general view of the surrounding landscape or building to show where the rock or decorative stonework is located. Next, take a close-up to show details of the specimen. You may find crystals, interesting colors, or patterns.

Write down the details of the location, the date, and a description of the subject. If your camera has adjustable settings, note the film speed, exposure, and lighting conditions, too, so that you will know which settings give the best results.

A scrapbook can contain any information or pictures connected with your hobby.

ROCK HOUND'S HINT
Look at the stones in your own backyard — you might find something interesting. Some of them may have been brought there from another area.

A QUICK GUIDE TO ROCK IDENTIFICATION

The best way to learn how to identify rocks, minerals, and fossils is to see as many examples as possible. Some museums will let you handle specimens, which is even better. The chart below will help you identify some of the most common types of rock. Simply follow the questions, answers, and information supplied.

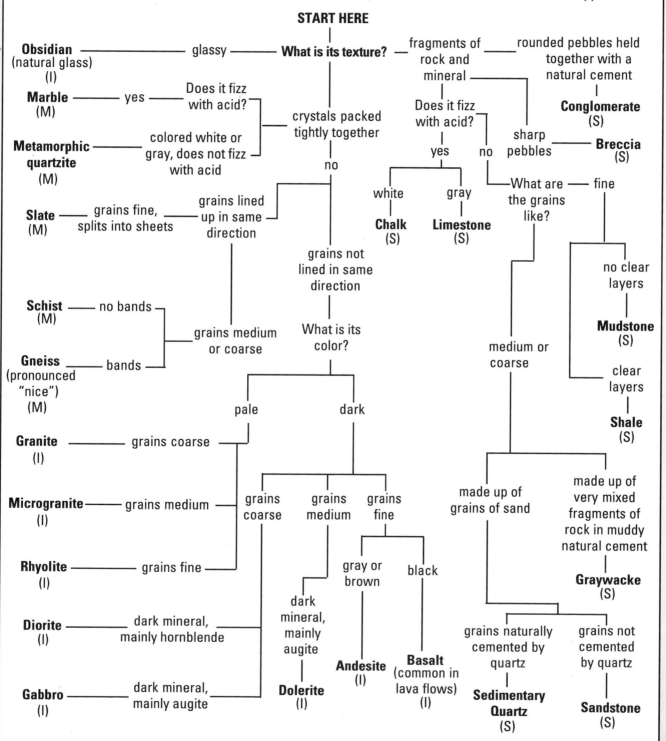

OUT AND ABOUT

As soon as you start collecting rocks and minerals, you will begin to notice them all around you. If you live in a place where the houses are more than 50 years old, you may find that the curbs and street pavement provide good examples to study. Curbs made of granite are easy to recognize by the three types of crystals they contain. If the pavement is dark-colored with few crystals, it is probably a volcanic rock. Modern curbstones and paving stones are usually made of concrete or brick, which are artificial or "man-made" rocks.

MAKING NOTES

Always make a note when you see something of interest, such as the rock and soil layers in a cutting being dug for a new road. In this way you will build up a picture of the geology of your home area. Do not enter dangerous areas such as construction sites. If you know of an interesting building project, why not write to the building company to see if you can visit the site and talk to the engineer?

THE ROCK HOUND'S CODE

Never trespass on private property.

Ask permission before removing specimens.

Take only a small piece of specimens you find.

Don't go near cliff tops.

Always wear a safety hat when near cliffs.

Respect wildlife such as plants and nesting birds.

ROCKS ON BUILDINGS

Looking up from the pavement, you will see that shop and office fronts often include polished rock slabs for decoration. In some cases you will find fossils, which show that the rock is almost certainly a sedimentary rock. Churches and public buildings often have statues or architectural decoration around the windows. These may be made of of stones that have been quarried locally. In some places all the older houses are built of stone, sometimes with stone tiles or slates on the roof.

AT THE CHURCH

A church is often one of the oldest buildings in a town. It is probably the best example of a building where rock has been used for construction and decoration. You may think that the graveyard is a depressing place, but there will be a good selection of rocks on display there. See if you can find out how quickly the different rock types used for headstones wear away in the wind and rain — the dates on the stones will help you make comparisons.

Look carefully at buildings to see the range of rocks used. There may be decorative marble, limestone around the windows, slate on the roof, granite or basalt pavement in front, and limestone steps and carvings.

Quarries, such as this large sand quarry, are ideal for looking at fresh material before it has weathered. You may find fossils as well as the sand, clay, or rock that is being extracted.

CLIFFS AND QUARRIES

The best places to find rocks are cliffs. They are dangerous places, and you should *never* go near them without an adult. Be careful when approaching cliffs, and avoid places where there have been landslides. Look for any warning signs. Many cliffs have clearly marked routes to a beach. As you go down them, look for rock strata. On the beach you might find fossils and minerals that have been weathered out of the cliff face. Sand and pebbles are worth collecting, too.

When you find some specimens, take them and your collecting equipment a safe distance from the cliff. You must *always* ask permission before removing specimens. Most land is private property. Also, many sites contain specimens that are protected by law, and you will be destroying part of the country's heritage by removing them.

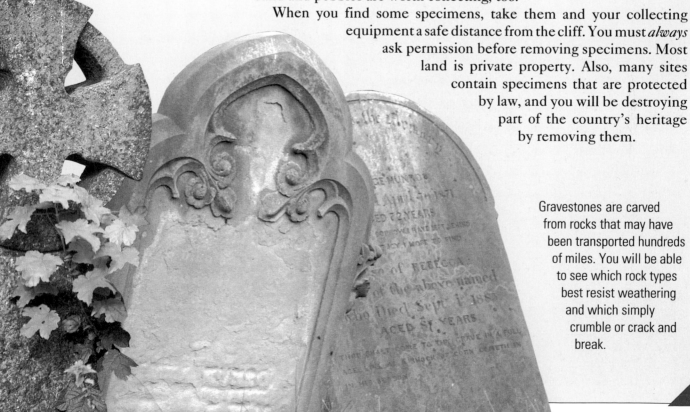

Gravestones are carved from rocks that may have been transported hundreds of miles. You will be able to see which rock types best resist weathering and which simply crumble or crack and break.

MAKING A SURVEY

Once you gain a greater knowledge of the rock types in your area, you may want to conduct a survey and make your own geological map. Don't be too ambitious at first — choose a small area close to home for your first attempt. Start by taping some clear film or tracing paper over a large-scale map of the area to be surveyed. Using a marker pen, draw an outline of the places that you intend to visit, including obvious contours, and features such as rivers, woods, and buildings. You can now transfer the outline map to a clipboard to take on your survey.

Geological maps (below) show the kinds of rocks that are under your feet, even if you cannot always see them.

YOUR OWN MAP

When you return from your survey, mark on the map where you found samples. Include a key to give the name or description of the sample. Mark any interesting building stones on your map. When you have finished you can keep the original map and your overlay together to give a permanent record.

ROCK HOUND'S HINT
Never go rock hunting alone. Always tell an adult where you are going and when you will return.

THE SURVEY

To carry out your survey, plan a route that crosses the ground several times. It is best to head up and down slopes in the landscape so that you cross the layers of rock as you go. Whenever you come to a bare rock, called an outcrop, take a sample and try to identify it. Also measure the dip of the layers. Number and label samples as you go, and keep a record of your findings and measurements.

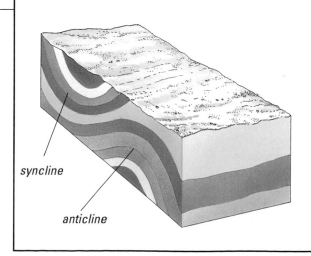

Some useful map symbols

/////	Landslide
o	Borehole, open shaft or well = DANGER!
20↑	The direction of strike, with the dip shown in degrees.
——	A line of contact between two rock layers, visible
– – – –	Estimated line of a hidden contact.
— — —	Fault line
LS	Limestone
SS	Sandstone
SH	Shale
DOL	Dolerite

Making a geological survey takes a lot of time and skill, but the result is very satisfying — your own geological map.

MAKING A CLINOMETER

A clinometer is used for measuring the incline, or slope, of rock layers. To make one, cut a notch in the middle of a plastic protractor, as shown in the diagram. Glue the protractor to a piece of wood about 8 in. wide, 6 in. long and at least ¾ in. thick. Next, cut out a pointer and fix it into the notch, where the protractor lines meet. This pointer should swing freely when you tilt the block of wood. Finally, paint over the protractor numbers and renumber it as shown in the picture below.

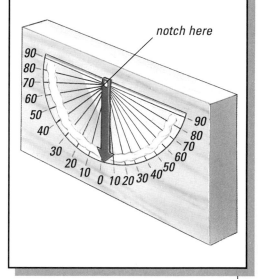

notch here

SYNCLINES AND ANTICLINES

These are two more features to include on your map. A syncline is a downward fold in a section of rock, and an anticline is an upward fold.

syncline

anticline

STRIKE AND DIP

Many rock layers are not horizontal. The angle at which a strata lies is called the dip. To measure the dip of a rock, place your clinometer on the sloping layer and swing it around until you get the maximum reading. The clinometer shown here is on a dip of about 20°. Use your compass to measure the direction of the dip. The strike of the rocks is a line at right angles (90°) to the dip.

direction of strike

angle of dip

direction of dip

PROPERTIES OF MINERALS

Minerals have special properties, and you will need to know some of them before you can start to identify the samples you collect. Important properties include color, luster, hardness, cleavage, and density, as well as the shapes of crystals and their habits (explained on page 64). Once you have worked out the properties of a sample, you can refer to the information on page 38 to help you identify it.

Goethite is usually yellow brown or black. This unusual specimen is iridescent — it shows the colors of the rainbow.

WHY SO MANY NAMES?
Some mineral names end in the letters "-lite," from the Greek word for rock, *lithos*. The first part of the name might refer to a property of the mineral (such as the blue mineral azurite, from azure, a shade of blue), or to places where they are found (such as Montmorillonite, from Montmorillon, France).

Some minerals have several names. This is because they have a number of forms, even though they are made up of the same type of particles. For example, the mineral quartz can have several colors. It is called amethyst when purple, citrine when yellow, and smoky quartz when dark brown or black. The colors are caused by traces of impurities.

Yellow sulfur (left) is found in areas of volcanic activity.

Fluorite (above) can be a difficult mineral to identify since it is found in several colors — the green crystals here are a common form. Blue sodalite (left) is very distinctive.

THE STREAK TEST

Looking at the color alone is not usually enough to identify a mineral. Sulfur, which is found near volcanoes, is always yellow. However, other minerals show a range of colors: feldspar crystals in granite can be white, cream, or brown, for example. To find a mineral's "true" color, scrape it across the unglazed back of a tile. The color of the mineral's powder mark is called the streak color — hematite's streak (right) is red-brown. The same mineral type will produce the same streak color on the tile even if several samples look different. This test only works for minerals that are softer than the unglazed tile. If the mineral is harder than the tile, use a steel file or nail to scratch the mineral. The powder on the scratch is the streak color.

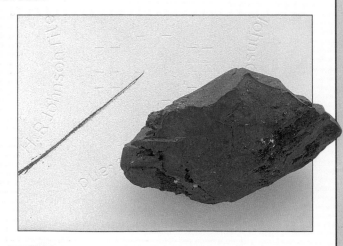

LUSTER

Many minerals have surfaces that are easy to recognize. Minerals containing metals have a metallic luster, a shiny surface that reflects light. Other minerals can have silky, glassy, or even greasy lusters. When you write notes about your mineral samples, describe the surface luster.

Pyrite has a shiny metallic luster and forms cubic crystals.

Serpentine has a greasy luster: this specimen has a fibrous (fiber-like) texture.

Talc is the softest mineral (1 on the Mohs scale). It has a greasy luster, and looks like soft chalk.

HARDNESS

This is one of the most useful properties of minerals to identify. The hardness scale, invented by the mineralogist Friedrich Mohs in 1822, is divided into 10 degrees of hardness. The rule is that any mineral can scratch another one of the same hardness or softer than itself. The hardest natural mineral, diamond, has a hardness value of 10 and can scratch anything else.

Using the examples of everyday objects shown in the Mohs scale, try scratching a mineral to measure its hardness. Move a sharp edge of the known object over the mineral to be tested. Now run a moistened fingertip over the surface to remove any loose powder and check to see if the mineral has been scratched. If you can scratch the mineral with a penknife blade but not with a copper coin, its hardness must be between 3.5 and 5.5. As your mineral collection grows, you will be able to build up a selection of the Mohs minerals for testing new finds. Mineral 10 may be a problem!

1 Talc
2 Gypsum
3 Calcite
4 Fluorite
5 Apatite
6 Orthoclase
7 Quartz
8 Topaz
9 Corundum
10 Diamond

2.5 Fingernail
3.5 "Copper" coin
5.25 Glass
5.5 Penknife
7.5 Steel file

CLEAVAGE AND FRACTURE

Some minerals and rocks can be split quite easily in particular directions. The mineral halite, a salt, is found as cubes. The cubes can be cleaved, or broken, into smaller cubes by using a hammer and sharp chisel. Many minerals will only break easily if they are hit in the right place.

Minerals and rocks will also fracture, or break unevenly. Quartz doesn't have a neat cleavage that you can see and fractures unevenly in all directions; the fracture is called conchoidal, or shell-like. Cleavage and fracture often helps to identify minerals and rocks.

Obsidian (above) is rich in the mineral silica. Like quartz (p. 40), it breaks like glass with a sharp shell-like edge, called a conchoidal fracture. Calcite crystals (right) are often found with a rhombic shape. You can break them into smaller rhombs.

THE FIZZ TEST

All carbonate minerals, such as calcite, fizz when treated with a drop of weak acid, such as vinegar. **Wear safety glasses and protective gloves when using acid.** Use a rock that you know to be a carbonate rock, such as limestone, and add a few drops of acid. Look for the fizz.

Now carefully add a few drops of vinegar to the sample being tested. Choose a part that contains nothing of special interest since the acid may damage the surface. Look for any evidence of fizzing. The gas being given off is carbon dioxide. Only carbonate minerals and rocks such as limestone give this test result.

ROCK HOUND'S HINT

Always wash your hands after handling minerals and carrying out tests. Also, keep your testing equipment clean so the remains of specimens tested previously don't confuse your results.

Mica (right) is well known for its cleavage into thin sheets. Some of them look like sheets of paper.

MAGNETISM

Some iron minerals are naturally magnetic. It's easy to identify them — just bring bring a compass near a sample, and the compass needle will point toward it.

Magnetite is a naturally magnetic iron ore. It can attract things made of iron, and compass needles will point toward it.

DENSITY

Minerals that are heavier than other minerals of the same size are said to have a higher density. Density is measured in metric units of grams per milliliter, and is also called SG, or specific gravity. Comparing the weight of a mineral with the weight of an equal volume of water gives its SG. An SG of 2 means that the mineral is two times as heavy as water.

The density test is complicated, but it provides useful information. First, weigh the mineral sample accurately in grams, say 150g. Next, measure the volume of the mineral. To do this, place some water in a metric measuring cup and note the volume reading. Carefully add the mineral and note the new reading. The difference between readings gives you the mineral volume, in milliliters, say 50ml. Use this formula to find the density:

$$\text{Density} = \text{mass in grams} \div \text{volume in milliliters}$$
$$= 150g \div 50ml$$
$$= 3g/ml$$

DENSITY

Find the mass in grams of the sample as accurately as you can by using metric scales or a balance. If you don't have one at home, ask you science teacher if you can use one at school.

Pour some water into a metric measuring cup until the water level is exactly opposite one of the scale marks. Note the volume reading in milliliters.

Add the sample that you have weighed previously. Make sure that no water is lost by splashing. Read the new higher water level. The difference between the second reading and the first reading is the volume of the rock sample. Then calculate the density.

If you can't take a sample home, try to guess its weight and volume. Compare it with an object or sample for which you know or can find out the density.

FLAME TESTS

Flame tests will show some other properties of minerals. Ask your science teacher at school to help you with flame tests. Flames and fumes can be dangerous, so be very careful.

FLAME TESTS

A gas flame is essential for carrying out some tests on rocks and minerals — school Bunsen burners are ideal for this purpose. When carrying out tests with flames and chemicals, always wear your safety glasses, and make sure that you have good ventilation. You should use pliers or tongs and pencil leads (*not* pencils), to place the samples safely in a hot flame. Have a ceramic tile ready to place hot things on safely.

FLAME COLORS

Many minerals contain metals that give a color to gas flames. Examples of this effect are the sparkling colors of a fireworks display and the bright orange-yellow color given to gas flames when salty water in a saucepan boils over, because salt contains the metal sodium.

The flame test works best if you use small, powdered samples. Large samples on the pencil lead are difficult to clean off for the next test. Using pliers to hold the lead, clean the end of a pencil lead (*not* a pencil) by heating it in the flame. Next, dip the lead into the powdered mineral sample and return it to the flame. Make a note of the first flash of color that you see. Different metals give characteristic flame colors that can be used to identify minerals:

Color of the flame	Metal present in mineral
dull red or orange	calcium
lilac	potassium
green-blue	copper
bright red	strontium
orange-yellow	sodium
yellow sparks	iron

calcium   *potassium*   *copper*   *strontium*   *sodium*

BORAX BEAD TESTS

The borax bead test is another test for showing what metals are present in a mineral. It uses borax, which is a white powder that melts easily in a gas flame. You will need a clean piece of stiff wire, called nichrome wire, with a loop in the end. Borax can be obtained from a supermarket, and wire from a hardware store. You can crush the bead between two coins to remove it from the wire loop after the test. If the beads are black, use less powder next time.

FLAMES

The color of the borax bead depends on where it is heated in the gas flame; the bead's color also changes when it cools. The tip of a blue gas flame is surrounded by oxygen gas in the air. This is called the "oxidizing" flame. When there is too little oxygen for the gas to burn completely, a yellow flame is produced. Inside this "reducing" flame, borax beads may turn different colors. The hot and cold bead colors are shown in the table below.

Borax beads can be used to identify the metal present in a mineral sample. Different metals give different bead colors.

BORAX BEAD TEST

Bend the end of a strong piece of wire into a small loop around the end of a sharp pencil lead. Heat the loop in the flame, holding the wire in some pliers. Dip the hot loop into powdered borax.

Return the borax to the flame and heat it until it swells up and then melts into a clear glassy bead.

Now touch the hot borax bead to a tiny piece of the mineral. Return it to the flame. Some minerals dissolve in the borax to create beautiful, colored glassy beads.

Oxidizing (blue) flame color		Reducing (yellow) flame color		Metal present
Hot	*Cold*	*Hot*	*Cold*	
yellow	green	green	green	chromium
green	blue	colorless to green	opaque red-brown	copper
yellow to orange	green to brown	bottle green	paler bottle green	iron
violet	red-brown	opaque gray	opaque gray	nickel
violet	red-violet	colorless	colorless	manganese

MINERAL DATA

The information on these pages will help you to identify some of the minerals you have collected. There are in fact over 2,500 minerals on Earth, but most of them are very rare, and the average collector is likely to find only about 300 of the most common and widespread. If you cannot find your mineral here, you will need to look in a field guide.

MINERAL DATA					
Mineral	**SG**	**Hardness**	**Flame**	**Acid**	**Streak**
Halite	2.5	2.5	yellow	no	no
Calcite	2.7	3.0	orange	yes	white
Gypsum	2.3	2.0	orange	no	white
Fluorite	3.2	4.0	orange	no	varies
Malachite	4.0	3.5	blue	yes	green
Quartz	2.6	7.0	no	no	white
Magnetite*	5.2	6.0	no	no	black
Galena	7.5	2.5	no	no	gray
Pyrite*	5.0	6.2	no	no	green/gray
Hematite*	5.0	varies	no	no	red

Note: All the minerals marked * are minerals containing iron, but only magnetite will affect a compass needle.

SPECIAL MINERAL PROPERTIES

Some minerals have unusual or special properties. For example, one variety of the mineral calcite, calcium carbonate, is called Iceland spar. The colorless crystals have the special property of making everything appear twice. If you place an Iceland spar crystal on some writing the words can be seen twice, an effect called double refraction. The effect is even more interesting if you rotate the crystal.

FLUORESCENCE

If you have a sample of fluorite you may find that it glows in ultraviolet (UV) light. Ultraviolet lights are used in tanning salons, and in discos to make colors glow in the dark. You may also have seen security inks that are invisible except when placed in UV light. Minerals such as fluorite that glow like this are said to be fluorescent.

Willemite (above) is a mineral that fluoresces in ultraviolet light. Light passing through a crystal of Iceland spar (below) is split into two so that you see a double image.

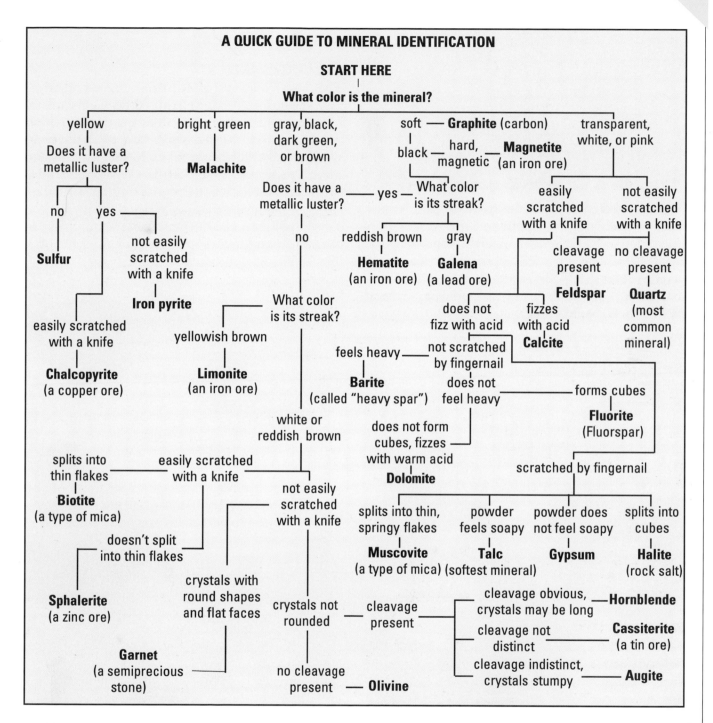

A QUICK GUIDE TO MINERAL IDENTIFICATION

START HERE

What color is the mineral?

- **yellow**
  - Does it have a metallic luster?
    - **no** → **Sulfur**
    - **yes**
      - easily scratched with a knife → **Chalcopyrite** (a copper ore)
      - not easily scratched with a knife → **Iron pyrite**
- **bright green** → **Malachite**
- **gray, black, dark green, or brown**
  - Does it have a metallic luster?
    - **yes** → What color is its streak?
      - reddish brown → **Hematite** (an iron ore)
      - gray → **Galena** (a lead ore)
    - **no** → What color is its streak?
      - yellowish brown → **Limonite** (an iron ore)
      - white or reddish brown
        - easily scratched with a knife
          - splits into thin flakes → **Biotite** (a type of mica)
          - doesn't split into thin flakes → **Sphalerite** (a zinc ore)
        - not easily scratched with a knife
          - crystals with round shapes and flat faces → **Garnet** (a semiprecious stone)
          - crystals not rounded
            - cleavage present
              - cleavage obvious, crystals may be long → **Hornblende**
              - cleavage not distinct → **Cassiterite** (a tin ore)
              - cleavage indistinct, crystals stumpy → **Augite**
            - no cleavage present → **Olivine**
- **soft** — **Graphite** (carbon)
  - **black** — hard, magnetic → **Magnetite** (an iron ore)
- **transparent, white, or pink**
  - easily scratched with a knife
    - cleavage present → **Feldspar**
      - does not fizz with acid
        - feels heavy → **Barite** (called "heavy spar")
        - not scratched by fingernail
          - does not feel heavy
            - does not form cubes, fizzes with warm acid → **Dolomite**
        - scratched by fingernail
          - splits into thin, springy flakes → **Muscovite** (a type of mica)
          - powder feels soapy → **Talc** (softest mineral)
          - powder does not feel soapy → **Gypsum**
          - splits into cubes → **Halite** (rock salt)
      - fizzes with acid → **Calcite**
      - forms cubes → **Fluorite** (Fluorspar)
  - not easily scratched with a knife
    - no cleavage present → **Quartz** (most common mineral)

RADIOACTIVITY

A few minerals are radioactive; that is, they give off streams of invisible particles. The special meter that can detect radioactivity is called a Geiger counter. The fuel for nuclear power stations comes from radioactive minerals.

Geiger counters make a clicking sound when they detect radiation from minerals such as pitchblende.

39

SILICA

The two most common elements in the Earth's crust are silicon and oxygen. Combined, they create silica (quartz), the most common mineral. When you go to the beach you usually walk on powdered silica: most people call it sand. A very resistant mineral, sand is all that is left of some types of rocks that have been broken up by weathering.

A SURPRISING VARIETY

Take some small plastic bags with you to the beach and start a sand collection. It is not until you have several samples from different beaches or sand dunes that you will realize how varied sand can be. The colors, sizes, and shapes of sand grains all give evidence about the original rocks. In some places you will be able to collect many varieties of sand from one location.

Collecting sand samples from the beach is very easy. You will be surprised at the variety of colors and grain sizes that you can find. Some sands are found in colored bands, so you might find several samples in one place.

CRYSTALLINE SILICA

The most famous varieties of silica are the quartzes used as gemstones in jewelry (p. 69). Colorless quartz is also known as rock crystal, purple quartz is amethyst, and the yellow variety is citrine. All of these minerals, as well as other silica varieties such as jasper, flint, and chert, can be found as pebbles on stony beaches. Many pebbles look rather disappointing since they have a white beach coating. When they are cracked open or polished, the full beauty of the minerals can be seen. If you test the hardness of silica pebbles, they will be harder than a penknife blade.

olivine sand

beach sand

volcanic sand

desert sand

rose quartz

citrine

smoky quartz

amethyst

a quartz geode

A SPECIAL TYPE OF SILICA

Some volcanoes produce a natural glass called obsidian. It is a rock but is very rich in silica. It is usually black and breaks with a curved surface, just like ordinary glass. If a volcano erupts violently, molten obsidian is thrown high into the air. As it cools and falls to Earth, it forms teardrop-shaped pieces, which are sometimes known as "Apache tears."

jasper

chert

agate

There are many varieties of silica. The colors of rose quartz and amethyst are produced by impurities in the silica. Geodes are cavities filled with crystals, and many fine amethysts have been found in geodes. Stony beaches often contain red or brown jasper pebbles. Agates are banded and look their best when polished.

FLINT TOOLS AND THE STONE AGE

Early peoples used flint to make cutting tools. You can try to recreate this early technology by shaping an arrow head or ax. If you are careful you may be able to produce your own Stone Age tools.

Collect some samples of flint and kneel on a thick cloth to protect your knees. Wear your safety glasses and some gloves, because flints are sharp. Hold one flint on the cloth and strike pieces off the edge using a second flint, called the flaking tool.

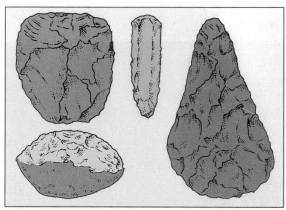

Small pieces can be chipped away to shape the flint. With some practice you will be able to produce sharp cutting edges like those made long ago. Stone Age peoples produced some very efficient flint tools and weapons, such as the hand ax, flaking tool, knife, and scraper shown here.

"Apache tears"

MINERAL WATERS

Have you ever noticed that the heating elements of electric kettles become covered with a white crust? This crust is calcium carbonate that had been dissolved in the water supply. You can quite easily show that the water supply contains dissolved minerals by filling a dark-colored dish with tap water and leaving the water to evaporate. Rings of the mineral crystals will be left on the dish.

Water has eroded and dissolved the rock to form the huge limestone pinnacles pictured above. Limestone caves (below) contain incredible landscapes of lakes, rivers, and columns. As water evaporates, stalactites grow from the roof as tubes.

UNDERGROUND CAVES

As rain water drains down through soil and rocks, it dissolves some of the minerals, especially the calcium carbonate of limestones. Sometimes streams dissolve a path through the rock. Gradually, large cave systems are formed underground.

The evaporation of the water inside the caves causes mineral crystals to form on the roof and floor. These stalactites and stalagmites grow very slowly, perhaps just a fraction of an inch each century. The surfaces of the rocks in the caves also become covered in dripstone (calcium carbonate again).

ROCK HOUND'S HINT
Never try to explore caves and potholes. They are very dangerous. If you want to see some limestone caves, go on a properly organized guided tour.

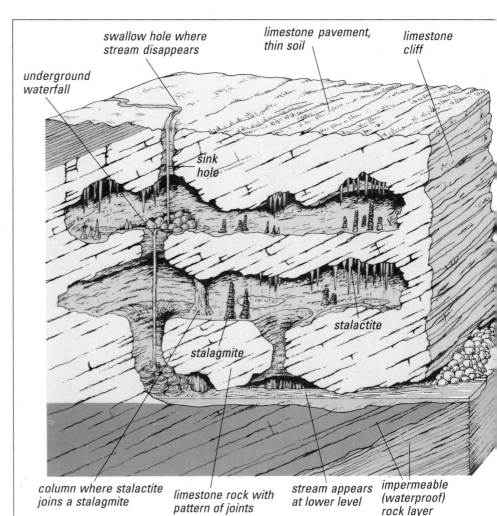

swallow hole where stream disappears

limestone pavement, thin soil

limestone cliff

underground waterfall

sink hole

stalactite

stalagmite

column where stalactite joins a stalagmite

limestone rock with pattern of joints

stream appears at lower level

impermeable (waterproof) rock layer

BOTTLED MINERAL WATERS

Many people like the taste of mineral waters and think that the dissolved materials may be good for their health. Look at the labels of some mineral water bottles, many of which give a list of the minerals that are dissolved in the water. Remember that most tap waters also contain minerals.

In some towns, there are health resorts where people can sample the mineral waters. Some of these spa towns have hot springs, and all sorts of claims are made about the benefits to people's health. Some natural springs produce radioactive waters, especially in volcanic areas. Travel guidebooks will help you locate some examples of spa towns.

When water dripping from above hits a cave floor, some of it evaporates and stalagmites grow upwards. When stalactites growing from the ceiling meet stalagmites, columns form.

TASTING SAMPLES

Get together with some friends and test some different water samples for taste. You could use tap water, different bottled waters, and distilled water, the purest form of all. Taste each sample, then, wearing a blindfold, see if you can correctly identify them again. Next, put the samples in order of taste, starting with the one you like most. Test the water samples for hardness. Hard water has a lot of calcium carbonate dissolved in it and will not easily form bubbles when shaken with soap powder. Using each sample in turn, see how much soap is needed to form a layer of bubbles that lasts for one minute.

WATER HARDNESS

Assemble some water samples in containers such as test tubes, along with some soap powder and a pair of tweezers. Using the tweezers, add some soap powder to the first water sample. Count and make a note of the number of grains of powder that you add.

Seal the tube and shake vigorously. Stop and see if the bubbles on the surface last for at least one minute. If not, add more powder and shake again. The harder the water sample, the more soap will be needed before the bubbles will last for one minute. Which water sample is the hardest?

METALS FROM THE ROCKS

Most metals are found as ore minerals, where the metal is combined with other materials. To use the metal, it has to be extracted, or separated, from the waste materials. Early peoples learned how to extract metals such as copper and tin from the ores using a process of heating called smelting. They heated the ore with charcoal to release the metal.

They soon discovered that if they smelted a mixture of copper and tin ores they could make bronze. Because it is a mixture, or alloy, of copper and tin, bronze is much stronger than either of them. Thousands of years ago, when people did not know how to smelt iron to make tools, bronze was used for jewelry, armor, and cutting blades. It was so important to the civilizations that used it that it has given its name to a period of history, the Bronze Age.

THE POWER TO SUCCEED

The very earliest miners probably used sharpened deer antlers as simple picks to extract minerals from rocks. Next came the use of flint axes and, later still, bronze cutting tools. It must have been a very hard life for the early miners. In some parts of the world people are still mining by hand, just relying on muscle power.

WATER POWER

Once the miners had brought the ore from the ground, it had to be separated from the gangue minerals, or waste materials. This was called dressing the ore. Originally the ore was broken up using hammers so that the valuable ore could be collected. Once water-powered hammers had been invented, tons of ore could be dressed in a day.

A big problem for miners was ground water leaking into the mine and flooding it. Early miners could only use buckets to try to keep their working area dry. The invention of steam engines (below) to pump water from deep underground allowed miners to work much deeper than before.

Bronze has been used for centuries to make tools and ornaments. Shown here are a Mycenean (Greek) dagger decorated with a scene of a lion hunt (made about 1300 B.C.), and a head sculpted in Nigeria (from about A.D. 1600).

44

iron ▲   aluminum ●   copper ◆

The map above shows some of the main areas where the important metals iron, copper, and aluminum are mined commercially.

Modern trains of mineral wagons are hauled by powerful locomotives built especially to carry the immensely heavy loads.

TAKING IT AWAY

Many mines were in remote places where there were no good roads. The miners needed to bring in supplies and take out the dressed ore ready for sale. In the early days of mining the best way to move heavy minerals was by boat, along the coast or rivers. In some areas, whole systems of canals were dug so that the valuable ores could be transported from the mines.

You can follow the development of new mines and the canals that served them by examining old maps. In some cases the mines were close to the sea so that simple mineral railroads could carry the ore to the harbor. The ore wagons of the first mineral railroads were dragged by horses, or even by men. However, once steam engines became small enough to be mobile, the ore wagons could be pulled by railroad engines.

INDUSTRIAL ARCHAEOLOGY

In many countries it is quite easy to spot abandoned mine sites with their distinctive engine houses, often built of the local granite rock. Nearby will be the dumps of waste material left by the miners.

ROCK HOUND'S HINT
When you travel always look out for evidence of old mineral workings, canals, and railroads. It will show you that you are in an area where interesting minerals can be found.

THE MOST IMPORTANT METAL

It is no accident that the Iron Age, when iron came to be used widely for tools, followed the Bronze Age. Although iron is the second most common metal in the Earth's crust, it needs a temperature of over 800°F for smelting. To get fires this hot, early metalworkers used charcoal to heat their furnaces. Whole forests were cut down to provide the charcoal.

The first iron bridge is still standing and is part of a museum of industrial heritage. It was so famous that the town is now called Ironbridge, England.

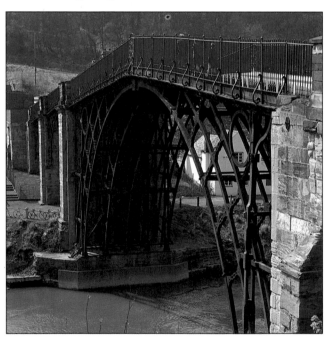

MODERN METHODS

In 1711 it was discovered that coke, made from coal, could be used instead of charcoal. This enabled the iron industry to develop new techniques for making items such as pots and pans. Soon, iron was being used to make bridges and railroads, and the Industrial Revolution began.

IRON ORES

You can find traces of iron minerals almost everywhere. When iron rusts, it combines with oxygen from the air to produce iron oxide, which is brown. This is the color to look for when collecting iron minerals. Most beach sands contain traces of iron oxide, and so have a brown color. Pure sand looks like granulated sugar and is colorless.

Magnetite is the easiest iron ore to identify since it is naturally magnetic. A piece of magnetite will attract the needle of a compass. Magnetite is also called lodestone since a piece of the ore will act as a simple compass if suspended from a thread. The ore is generally black with a metallic luster.

Another ore of iron is hematite, which can be red or black. This is one case where the streak test for minerals is invaluable. Different-colored samples of hematite all give a similar streak color, red-brown, on a tile.

yellow limonite

brown limonite

The brown and yellow earthy forms of limonite (above) are known as ochers, and they are used to make paint. Sienna and umber, which contain aluminum, iron, and manganese, are also pigments.

WEATHERING

New iron minerals form as a result of weathering (the effects of the weather). One example is limonite, which has been used for thousands of years as a pigment, or coloring. Early artists used earth that had been colored by limonite and other mineral deposits to provide a range of colors, mostly yellows, browns, reds, and black. The color of limonite depends on the size of the mineral grains, so many different shades can be produced.

IRON FROM OUTER SPACE

Meteorites are pieces of material from outer space that have been captured by the Earth's gravity. Most meteorites burn up as they fall through the atmosphere, but some larger ones reach the surface. Many meteorites are made of the metals iron or nickel. Geologists are interested in meteorites because they provide evidence about the make-up of planetary material from elsewhere in the solar system. When very large meteorites land, large craters are formed.

Prehistoric people made paints by mixing earth pigments and vegetables with water or animal fat. Some caves, such as those at Altamira in Spain (above), have walls that were painted more than 15,000 years ago. Colors, such as blue, came from minerals like azurite (below), which contains copper.

There are some stony meteorites, but most are made of iron and nickel. You will need to be very lucky to find a meteorite, but you might see one falling through the night sky.

FOOL'S GOLD

Iron pyrite is a beautiful golden yellow mineral that many collectors have mistaken for gold. The name pyrite comes from the Greek words *pyrites lithos*, which mean "stone that strikes fire." Pyrite will sometimes spark when struck on a lump of iron.

azurite

Iron pyrite, or "fool's gold" (right), looks like gold and forms some wonderful crystals, but it will not make your fortune.

EXTRACT YOUR OWN METALS

Most metals are found combined with other materials. For example, tin combines with oxygen to form cassiterite. For us to be able to use them, these metals must be extracted from their ores, or naturally occurring minerals. A few metals, such as gold and copper, are found in a pure form. They are called native metals.

Gold is a native metal. If you find gold nuggets they will be pure gold, which never rusts like iron and so always retains its shiny appearance.

GOLD FEVER

Nobody knows how gold was first discovered, but it seems likely that gold nuggets were first found in the bed of a stream. This is because minerals are sometimes washed out of rocks as rivers flow over them. Since gold is very dense, it collects in hollows in the stream bed. In the 19th century, gold prospectors separated gold dust from sand and gravel by panning — swirling dirt and water in a pan. Try taking a pan with you when you go to the seashore. Sometimes dense minerals are washed onto a beach by streams and can be found by panning. It is also worth digging a hole in the sand and trying the panning technique on material from a lower level. You may even strike gold!

HOW TO GO PANNING

To go panning, you will need a shallow circular dish or old frying pan without the handle. Add a mixture of sand and something dense (heavy) to represent the gold, such as lead shot or iron filings. Pour in some water and swirl the mixture around. Before the water has stopped swirling, pour out most of the mixture. Any dense material should be left at the base of the pan. You can pick up magnetic metals with a magnet.

LEACHING ORES

When minerals are separated from a rock by dissolving them in a liquid, it is called leaching. You will need to find a metallic ore to see how this happens. The easiest ones to use are iron or copper minerals, both of which are common.

Wearing safety goggles and gloves, break up about 4 oz. of mineral wrapped in cloth by hitting it with a hammer. Put the broken mineral into a filter funnel (lined with filter paper), and support the funnel in the mouth of a clear jar or bottle.

Add some strong vinegar, the leaching solution. As the liquid drains through the mineral, some of the metallic material will dissolve. The leachate, the liquid that drains through, will be blue-green if copper is present and yellow-brown for iron. You may need to pour the same liquid through more than once for the leaching to be successful.

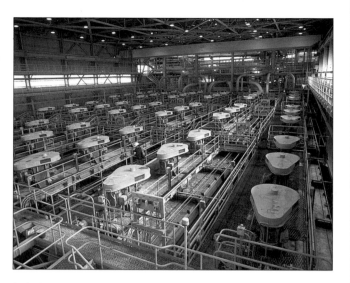

In industry, large amounts of material must be treated to remove the mineral from the waste rock. For example, some copper ores contain less than one percent copper, the other 99 parts in 100 being waste. Therefore a simple method is needed to concentrate the valuable part of the ore. The discovery of froth flotation (above) has solved the problem.

FROTH FLOTATION

The process of froth flotation is used to concentrate valuable minerals. To see how it is done, mix some powder from sharpening a pencil (to represent the mineral) with some sand and water. Add a *little* liquid disinfectant and blow *gently* through a straw into the mixture. Do *not* drink the mixture. You will find that the mineral grains stick to the bubbles and rise to the surface of the mixture.

FOSSILS: AN AMAZING VARIETY

Everyone has seen pictures of dinosaur fossils and probably reconstructions as well. In some cases scientists have only a few bones from which to deduce what the creature looked like. You are unlikely to find dinosaur bones, but there are many other types of fossils, just waiting for the collector.

AMMONITES AND BELEMNITES

Ammonites are very common fossils, both as shells and as impressions in rocks. Most ammonites have curved shells, often with distinctive patterns on them. When perfect specimens are sliced in half you can see a series of chambers inside. Belemnite fossils are all that remain of creatures similar to a modern cuttlefish. Belemnites look rather like rifle bullets.

Both ammonites and belemnites are common fossils because they had hard parts that could be preserved easily. The soft parts of cuttlefish — the tentacles, for example — usually leave no traces in the rocks. Impressions left in soft sediments that eventually hardened into rock are called trace fossils.

Fossils such as *micraster* (below), a form of sea urchin, are often found in chalk. They are shaped in a five-fold pattern like starfish. Sand dollars (below right) are related to sea urchins, too.

Amber can preserve creatures for millions of years, in perfect detail. The wasp on the left was caught with its prey, a fly, over 30 million years ago. Deeply colored amber will polish well and is valued as a gem.

AMBER

Pine trees produce a sticky resin, and insects often become trapped in it. When this resin hardens it can become preserved as a fossil known as amber. Some specimens of amber contain insects from millions of years ago, perfectly preserved.

Bullet-shaped belemnites (right) and curly ammonites (bottom right) are found in many varieties.

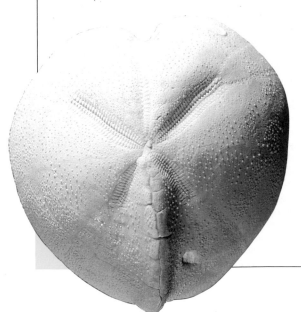

SEA URCHINS AND SEA LILIES

In chalk you can often find fossilized sea urchins. Usually the spines have been lost, although today's sea urchins show how the creatures might have looked millions of years ago. Sea lilies, or crinoids, are also common as fossils. The top part, or calyx, was supported on a long stem fixed to the sea bed. It is possible to find "crinoidal" limestones where the rock is studded with pieces of broken crinoid stem. They look like little flat beads made of stone.

TRILOBITES

Among the oldest fossils to be found are the trilobites. They looked like giant wood lice but were sea creatures that lived on the seabed. Sometimes you can find their tracks in the rock, as trace fossils.

Fossil coral (left) is formed from the hard parts of ancient corals.

The descendants of the fossil sea urchins (right) still live in the sea today. Often the fossil ones have lost their spines.

There are many species of trilobites (above and below) to find.

Crinoids (left) must have been very common since some limestones are made almost completely of their remains.

Fossil fish and shark teeth (right) are sometimes found in large numbers. They are hard, and preserved well as fossils when the rest of the body disappeared.

51

CASTS AND MOLDS

Sometimes the remains of a creature become covered in sediment. As the sediment slowly hardens into rock, the remains may rot away completely. This leaves a hole in the rock the same shape as the creature. This is called a mold. The people buried in the Roman city of Pompeii by the volcanic eruption of A.D. 79 left molds.

When plaster of Paris is poured into a mold, the original shape can be seen. The plaster forms a cast of the fossil. This process also happens naturally when minerals dissolved in ground water collect in a fossil mold. When the rock is broken open, there is a cast inside, perhaps made of calcite or quartz. None of the original material remains.

TRACKS

There are many examples of tracks left by creatures long ago. Fossilized footprints from both dinosaurs and people have been found in rocks. In fact, some dinosaurs are known only from their tracks as no bones have been found yet.

Just like footprints left in the sand, dinosaurs left tracks (above) that are sometimes preserved in hard rock.

Splitting a block of limestone revealed this ammonite (above). The shell along the outer spiral has split away. Inside, calcite crystals have grown into the space where the ammonite's fleshy body lived. Often a fossil is partly covered by rock (left). With great care the covering can be scraped or dissolved away to show the full detail (p. 15).

Most wood rots after trees have died, but sometimes the wood is replaced by minerals and an amazing fossil forest is formed (right).

FOSSIL CASTS

Place a 1 in. deep layer of damp sand in a shallow tray to represent a soft sediment. Press a fossil, seashell, or other small object into the sand to make a clear impression.

Mix some plaster of Paris with water to form a smooth paste, and pour it over the sand, making sure that the impression is completely covered. Wait until the plaster has set hard.

Carefully lift the plaster and examine the cast of the impression in the sand. Many fossils are preserved in a similar way.

PETRIFIED WOOD

Coal is one example of fossilized plants, but there are some others. When forests become covered by water or fallen trees become waterlogged, the wood is sometimes preserved intact. However, silica in ground waters can replace the woody material, leaving a quartz fossil. Some of this petrified, or fossilized, wood is harder than steel, and the tree rings can still be counted. Museums display polished slices of petrified wood.

LEAF CASTS

You can also make casts of leaves using clay as a base. First, make a bed with the clay, then cover it with petroleum jelly to prevent the clay and plaster of Paris from sticking together. Press a ribbed leaf into the clay to make an impression.

Remove the leaf and build up some clay walls, smeared with petroleum jelly, to hold in the plaster. Pour in the mixed plaster and leave it to set.

HOW OLD ARE THEY?

The serious study of fossils did not start until the 19th century. Although fossils had been known to people for centuries, they were not originally recognized as being the remains of living things. Even in the 19th century, some naturalists claimed that it was simply a coincidence that fossils looked like some living creatures or plants.

A SERIOUS SUBJECT
One of the first geologists to take fossils seriously was Frenchman Georges Cuvier. His studies in the early 19th century resulted in paleontology — the study of past living things — being recognized as a separate science. It was Cuvier who identified and named the extinct flying reptile pterodactyl.

THE USE OF SCIENCE
Today the study of fossils is aided greatly by technology. There are ways in which the ages of rocks and fossils can be calculated, by measuring traces of radioactive material in them. Once the age of a fossil is known, it can be used to date other rocks that contain the same type of fossil. Fossils also provide evidence about the environment and climate of the times the organisms were alive.

This table divides up the Earth's history into smaller parts, each with its own name and age of millions of years ago. The details of the table are constantly being changed as scientists learn more.

THE STRATIGRAPHICAL TABLE
Even though modern technology can help scientists, geologists have to make certain assumptions about the ages of rocks and fossils. One is known as the Law of Superposition. It says that when examining strata, younger rocks will be above older ones, since they formed more recently.

Using the study of strata, scientists have divided the Earth's history into periods of time. The information is contained in a diagram called the stratigraphical table (below). This geological time-scale took many years to develop. Studies of rock strata from one area can be used to date rocks, and the fossils they contain, in other areas.

ERA	PERIOD	EPOCH		millions of years ago
	Quaternary			2
				5
Cenozoic	Tertiary	Neogene	Holocene Pliocene Pleistocene Miocene	25
			Oligocene	38
		Paleogene	Eocene	55
			Paleocene	65
Mesozoic	Cretaceous			
				146
	Jurassic			
				208
	Triassic			245
Paleozoic	Permian			290
	Carboniferous	Pennsylvanian		
		Mississippian		363
	Devonian			409
	Silurian			439
	Ordovician			510
	Cambrian			570
	Precambrian			610

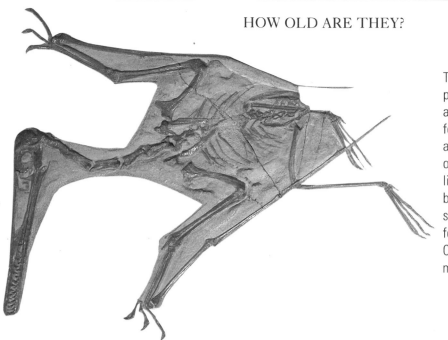

The pterodactyl or pterosaur (don't pronounce the "p") was a flying reptile and is very rare as a fossil. Study of the fossil on the left shows the light bones and traces of wing material stretched over them. Pterodactyls may have rested like modern bats, upside down on tree branches or rocks. Some features are similar to modern birds. Pterodactyl fossils are of the Jurassic and Cretaceous periods, about 100–200 million years old.

THE FIRST FOSSILS

Scientists believe that the Earth is about 4.6 billion years old. The earliest traces of fossil life in the rocks are much more recent than this, however, because only some things are likely to be preserved as fossils. Shells and bones are hard and often found as fossils, but the early animals were like soft worms and jellyfish and so have not often been preserved. Nevertheless, there is evidence for simple creatures like algae from nearly 2 billion years ago.

As we come closer to the present, more complicated living things begin to appear in the fossil record. Almost all the common fossils that you will find date from the last 600 million years.

A GIANT JIGSAW

Sometimes fossils of land creatures of the same species and age are found on opposite sides of an ocean. How did they get there? One explanation is that all the land on the Earth was originally joined together. A theory called plate tectonics suggests that land masses drift slowly across the Earth's surface. Over millions of years they have traveled great distances. Thus continents that are now separated by water could once have been joined together.

175 million years ago

300 million years ago

50 million years ago

You can draw Earth's history like a clock face (above). It shows in which order life appeared on the planet. There is good evidence that the shapes and positions of the land masses (left) have changed greatly over that time.

MAKING YOUR NAME

Fossil hunting can be great fun, and the finders may even make history. One fossil hunter who became famous was an English schoolgirl from Dorset, England. Mary Anning was only 11 years old when she discovered the first fossil *Ichthyosaurus*, a large sea-living creature, in 1810. She went on to make many more fossil discoveries and is commemorated in a church stained-glass window.

THE FINDER'S NAME

Some people who find new types of creatures are lucky enough to have the creatures named after them. For example, the dinosaur *Protoceratops andrewsi* ("Andrews' early horned head") was named after Roy Chapman Andrews. He was the leader of an American expedition that found over 100 *Protoceratops* skeletons in Mongolia in the early 1920s. Many other dinosaurs are named after their finders.

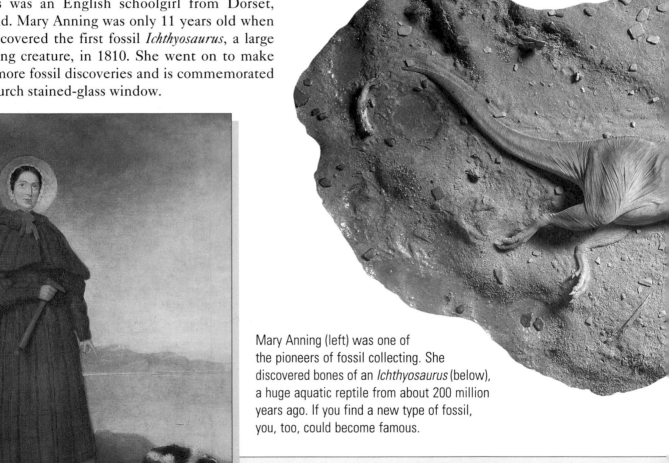

Mary Anning (left) was one of the pioneers of fossil collecting. She discovered bones of an *Ichthyosaurus* (below), a huge aquatic reptile from about 200 million years ago. If you find a new type of fossil, you, too, could become famous.

The coelacanth has been a very successful survivor. It is known to have existed for millions of years.

Careful study of the fossils of *Baryonyx walkeri* ("Walker's big claw") has led to a reconstruction (left) to show how the creature might have looked. It was named in part after its finder, amateur collector William Walker.

LIVING FOSSILS

There are some creatures described as living fossils. These are ones that are known from the fossil record but were thought to be extinct. One of the most famous is a fish called a coelacanth. Fossils of coelacanths have been found in rocks as old as 400 million years and as young as 65 million years. After this, there was no evidence of the coelacanth surviving until a living specimen was caught by fishermen off the coast of Madagascar in 1938. Since then other specimens of this living fossil have been found.

CAREFUL RESEARCH

When you start a fossil collection of your own, find out as much as possible about fossils from local museums and books. Once you become familiar with the range of fossils in a particular area, you will know when something unusual turns up. Some people have made their livings as fossil collectors.

A knowledge of the main rock types will be a great help when you are collecting. Don't forget, there is little point in searching for fossils in igneous rocks such as granite since there are none. The main types of sedimentary rock may provide you with fossils for your collection.

Bones can be joined together to form a skeleton, even if some of the bones are missing. This is a reconstruction of *Triceratops*, "three-horned head," whose massive bone skull preserves well as a fossil.

FOSSILS AND OIL

The world's first oil well was drilled in Pennsylvania in 1859. This was the start of one of the world's biggest industries, the oil industry. Oil is used to generate the electricity used in homes and businesses, and for transportation. It is also used to make most of our plastics, rubbers, and synthetic fibers ("man made" materials such as nylon).

OIL EXPLORATION

In some parts of the world, oil and natural gas escape naturally at the surface of the ground. In the Middle East there are "eternal fires," places where escaping gas has been burning naturally for thousands of years. On some seashores oil seeps out naturally from the rocks. Obviously, signs like this give geologists strong indications that more oil and natural gas are buried underground. Some of the deposits of oil are under the seabed, such as those in the North Sea. Many more, such as the huge Texan and Middle Eastern oil fields, are under dry land.

Drilling oil wells is very expensive, often costing millions of dollars for a single well. Therefore geologists need as much evidence as possible of the presence of large quantities of oil before starting to drill. If oil is suspected, rock samples are collected and examined, and surveys of the whole area are carried out. If the prospects for finding oil look good, holes are drilled to examine the rocks underground.

Oil and natural gas, such as methane, are usually found together. Sometimes waste gas must be "flared off" (above) before the oil can be transported safely for processing at oil refineries.

PROSPECTING METHODS

Before drilling an oil well, geologists must survey the rocks to see if they are of the right type and structure to contain oil. In one method (below), a small explosion is used to send shock waves down to the rock layers below. Microphones detect the

Nodding donkeys (right) are pumps that bring oil to the surface from the underground oil field. Sometimes microfossils (below) provide evidence of oil deposits.

LOOKING FOR FOSSILS

The drills provide both rock chippings and core samples for further study. Since the samples are small, it is unlikely that ordinary fossils will be present. Luckily there are other types of fossils that are of great interest to the oil geologist. These are the microfossils (very small fossils) that can be present in rock chippings in great numbers.

Extracting and studying microfossils is a job for the experts. The rock samples must be crushed to release the fossils, and microscopes are needed to examine them in detail. One type of microfossil, known as foraminifera, is found very widely in oil-bearing rocks. Since oil and gas can move through the rocks over long periods of time, the fossils may still be there even though the oil has escaped. Therefore finding some foraminifera in the rock does not *prove* that oil is there as well, but it provides more evidence that the area being searched is a good one.

MATCHING ROCKS

Plant spores are another type of microfossil. In an area where coal or oil has been found, geologists try to match the types of plant spores with spores in rocks of a similar age in another area. The new area may be worth investigating for oil deposits if the microfossils in the rocks are the same.

Geologists use special drills to bring up rock cores. They can then study the rock samples, such as this conglomerate.

patterns of echoes, which give information about the rock structure. Vibrosis (below) is used in built-up areas. In this method, heavy weights are dropped on the ground to set up the shock waves.

CRYSTALS

Have you ever fractured a bone? If you have, then you've probably had an X ray. Scientists have used X rays in the same way to examine solids to find out about the arrangement of particles — called atoms — inside them. A crystal is a solid that is made up of atoms arranged in an orderly, regular pattern. The edges of perfect crystals are straight, and the angles between the edges are the same size for the same kinds of crystal.

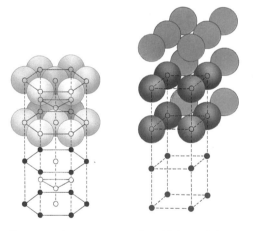

These diagrams show two ways in which particles are arranged in a regular and repeating way in a crystal. On the left is a hexagonal arrangement, on the right a cubic one.

CRYSTAL SYSTEMS

Crystals can be described according to their shapes. The shapes of crystals reflect the arrangement of atoms inside them. There are seven crystal shapes or "systems": cubic, tetragonal, hexagonal, orthorhombic, monoclinic, triclinic, and trigonal. When identifying minerals that are crystalline, it is helpful to know which crystal system the mineral represents. Many samples that you collect will not have perfectly formed crystals, so you will have to make an intelligent guess!

BUBBLE RAFTS

One way of showing how atoms arrange themselves in crystals is to use a bubble raft. Make some soapy water in a shallow dish and, using a straw, blow enough bubbles to cover the surface. You will find that the bubbles form regular arrangements and patterns. Using a ruler, move rows of bubbles past each other.

CRYSTAL SYSTEMS

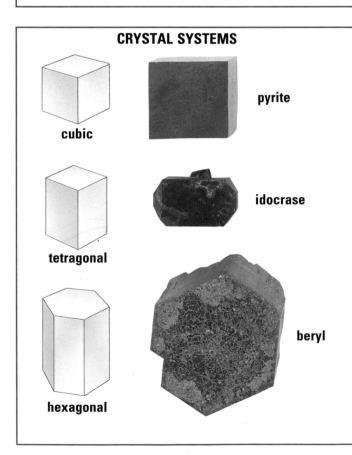

cubic

pyrite

tetragonal

idocrase

hexagonal

beryl

How easy is it? Use straws of different diameters to make bubbles of different sizes. In crystalline alloys, mixtures of metals, the "bubbles" will be of different sizes, too. See how this makes it more difficult for the layers of bubbles to slide past each other. This is why alloys are stronger than pure metals.

CRYSTAL MODELS

You can try making some model crystals to see the ways in which the separate atoms are arranged inside. Drop marbles or ball bearings a few at a time into a cardboard frame. Even though the marbles are dropped or poured in a random manner, they will line up to produce a regular pattern. The atoms will have the same angles between them. It is easiest to start with a square frame, but you can also try frames of different shapes.

Make a cardboard frame, about 5 in. along each side, to hold some marbles. If you use larger objects as "atoms," you will need to use a bigger tray, too.

Pour a stream of marbles into the frame from just above the center point. Collect any marbles that escape and pour them in again. Can you see a pattern forming?

Here is one result of dropping some marbles into a square tray. If real atoms behave like this, you can see how a regular structure is built up, forming a beautiful crystal.

barite

orthorhombic

gypsum

monoclinic

axinite

triclinic

siderite

trigonal

GROWING CRYSTALS

It is very easy to grow crystals. Some crystals don't need much help at all. For example, crystals of calcium carbonate grow inside kettles when they are heated. Or you can leave different water samples to evaporate on saucers, and use a magnifying glass to examine the solids left behind. The homegrown crystals described on these pages can be very beautiful and grow to a large size if you are patient. Blue copper sulfate crystals always grow very well, but there are lots of others you can try. Alums come in different colors although the crystal shape is the same. You can even grow one alum crystal on top of a different-colored one.

You will probably never grow a crystal like this! It is a beautiful crystal of apatite growing on albite, a form of feldspar. Apatite is the main mineral found in bones and teeth.

HOMEGROWN CRYSTALS

The best crystals take a long time to grow. You can use copper sulfate for blue crystals, magnesium sulfate for colorless ones, or the alums for a variety of colors. All of these chemicals are likely to be found in a chemistry set, or a pharmacist may agree to sell you some, with your parents' agreement.

The technique for growing the crystals is the same in each case. Dissolve as much of the powdered solid in hot water as you can. Stir all the time to help the solid dissolve. Filter the mixture (through coffee filter paper, for example) to take out any undissolved solid. Leave the saturated solution (a solution that is full of the dissolved material) to cool and evaporate. After a few days crystals will form and grow.

BIGGER STILL

If you want to make some *very* large crystals, choose a well-shaped crystal from the experiment above. Tie a thread to it and suspend it in the same solution, adding extra saturated solution as it evaporates. If you carry on long enough you may need a trash can to hold the growing crystal and its solution.

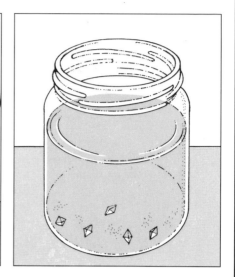

HYPO CRYSTALS

You should wear your safety glasses for this experiment. Hypo is short for sodium thiosulfate, a chemical used by photographers. Place about ½ oz. of hypo crystals in a test tube (ask your science teacher if you can borrow one of these) and add a few drops of water. Gently warm the mixture over a flame (below left), until you see a clear liquid. Be careful not to boil the liquid or the experiment may not work. Set aside the mixture to cool without any disturbance.

When the tube is completely cold again, add one hypo crystal as a seed crystal (below right). What happens around the edges of the seed crystal? What do you notice about the temperature?

COMMERCIAL USES

Very pure crystals are grown for use in industry. Crystals are needed in lasers and for silicon chips, the material needed to make electronic circuits for computers and calculators. Ruby crystals are grown and made into low-friction bearings for mechanical watches.

Special crystals are also needed to make holograms, the pictures that seem to be in 3-D, or three dimensions. Holograms are used as security markings for bank credit cards.

CRYSTAL HABITS

Unfortunately, natural crystals often don't form as perfectly as the ones you can grow, because they don't grow in perfect conditions. Their shape can vary depending on the development of the individual faces. Also, large single crystals are comparatively rare. You are much more likely to find minerals as large groups of crystals, called aggregates.

Some of the names that scientists have given these crystal shapes are quite difficult to remember. The important thing for a collector to note is what a specimen looks like. You can look up the proper scientific description in a book later, when you are writing up your notes. On the next page are some of the crystal forms, or habits, with their scientific names.

Artificial crystals (such as this ruby, right) can be grown using a freezing technique. The crystals have been used in lasers to create holograms (above). The silicon chip (far right) is a section of an artificial crystal used to make integrated circuits for computers.

SOME CRYSTAL HABITS

Description	Appearance	Scientific Name
sheets	sheets that can easily be split	foliated
spheres	like round balls	globular
grapes	formed of rounded masses, like a bunch of grapes	botryoidal
columns	like columns	columnar
hairy	like a dense mass of hair or fiber	fibrous
fernlike	looks like branches of a fern or tree	dendritic
blades	thin, narrow strips	bladed
netted	like the mesh of a net	reticulated
radiating	spreading outward from a single point	radiating
spiky	lots of needles, like a porcupine	acicular

Pyrophyllite is a very soft glassy mineral that can be found in radiating form (shown here).

The spiky needles in the quartz (below) are crystals of rutile.

Crystals of marcasite are often shaped like spears (below).

Wolframite (below) is an ore of the metal tungsten. Wolframite crystals are long, bladed prisms.

Some crystals grow as "twins," identical or mirror images of each other. This is a calcite "butterfly" twin.

Actinolite (below) is a mineral that is rich in iron. It has long bladed crystals.

This fine specimen of native copper has an irregular dendritic, or branching, habit.

CRYSTALS AROUND US

Crystals are found not just in minerals and rocks, but all around us. In fact, virtually all naturally occurring solids are crystalline.

CRYSTALLINE FOOD

Almost every day of your life you eat some crystals. Table salt is crystals of sodium chloride. Salt crystals are cubic in shape. You can examine some different types of salt with a hand lens to compare the crystal shapes. Sometimes the edges of salt crystals become rounded during the manufacturing process.

In many parts of Europe there are remains of Roman salt works. Salt water, called brine, was heated in large salt pans to evaporate the water and leave salt crystals behind. Where the weather was warm enough, the heat of the sun was used to evaporate seawater. This method of producing salt is still used in places such as Australia and Brittany in France.

SWEET CRYSTALS

Another crystalline food is sugar. Sugar is not a mineral — it comes from plants, not rocks — but the particles inside it are arranged in the same way as a mineral's. See how many different sugar crystals you can find at home or at the supermarket.

sugar

Salt crystals (above) are cubic, although their size may vary. They can be extracted from brine in salt pans (below left). Although sugar is often sold as a fine powder, there are lots of crystalline varieties (below). Colored crystals may be raw cane sugar (brown) or may have had colors added to them.

sugar

sugar

SOME USES OF CRYSTALS

Metals are crystalline, although it is not always easy to see the crystal structure. One example of the use of metal crystals is called galvanizing. This is a process of putting a layer of zinc crystals onto iron items, such as nails, to prevent the iron from rusting. The galvanized iron used to make wheelbarrows or buckets has large zinc crystals on its surface.

Early radio sets were called crystal wireless sets. In order to pick up a radio transmission, the user had to position a fine wire in exactly the right place on a crystal of galena. The wire was referred to as a cat's whisker because it was so thin, and getting the crystal set to work was quite an art.

Ice crystals always form regular shapes of repeating units. It is often said that no two snowflakes are the same!

SEEDING THE SKY

During a drought, aircraft can be used to seed rain clouds with silver iodide crystals to encourage raindrops to form. This is a very expensive way to water the ground!

Did you know that crystals fall out of the sky in cold weather? Snowflakes are crystals. You can study them by collecting them on glass microscope slides that have first been cooled in a freezer. You can also grow ice crystals by putting a piece of damp cloth in a freezer — choose a dark-colored surface so that the crystals show up clearly.

A HARD SURFACE

Silica (quartz) is one of the minerals found in granite. With corundum powder it can be used to make sandpaper. The hard silica and corundum crystals smooth other surfaces. Artificial crystalline materials, such as silicon carbide, can be used to make these abrasive papers, too.

Corundum is made of aluminum oxide, the same chemical that forms rubies. Corundum is useful as an abrasive.

Diamonds (top) are used to stud the tips of dentist drills and for rock drills. Galena crystals (above) were used in early crystal radio sets. Galena is one of the main ores of lead and often forms beautiful cubic crystals.

DIAMONDS ARE FOREVER

In industry (left), diamonds are used for cutting other hard materials. Industrial diamonds can now be made artificially.

The hardest natural mineral is diamond. On the Mohs scale it has a hardness of 10. It is this property of diamonds that inspired the famous advertising slogan "diamonds are forever." Yet diamonds are made of the common element carbon. As long ago as 1695, scientists in Florence, Italy demonstrated that diamonds disappear when heated in air. When they burn they produce very expensive carbon dioxide gas!

Diamonds have been used in jewelry (right) for centuries, either on their own or with other gemstones.

HOT AND HARD

Diamonds are formed under conditions of high temperatures and pressures. They are mined in ancient volcanic pipes, the remains of extinct volcanoes where these conditions would have existed. By reproducing these conditions, it is possible to make artificial diamonds from another form of carbon called graphite. (Graphite is the material from which pencil leads are made.) Diamonds have occasionally been found in meteorites from outer space.

DIAMONDS AT WORK

Diamonds are widely used in industry. Since they are so hard, diamonds are used for the cutting edges of rock drills and for polishing other hard materials. In fact, only about 20 percent of all diamonds are used in jewelry. The largest diamond ever found was the Cullinan stone from South Africa. It weighed 3,106 carats, the equivalent of about 1⅓ pounds. It was presented to King Edward VII of Britain in 1907.

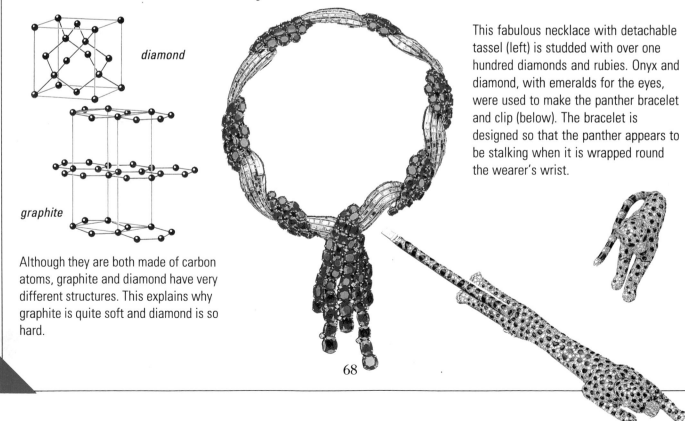

diamond

graphite

Although they are both made of carbon atoms, graphite and diamond have very different structures. This explains why graphite is quite soft and diamond is so hard.

This fabulous necklace with detachable tassel (left) is studded with over one hundred diamonds and rubies. Onyx and diamond, with emeralds for the eyes, were used to make the panther bracelet and clip (below). The bracelet is designed so that the panther appears to be stalking when it is wrapped round the wearer's wrist.

Uncut diamonds look very different from the cut and polished ones used in jewelry. Diamonds can be cut using other diamonds to make finished gems.

SEMIPRECIOUS STONES

You may not find any diamonds for your collection but there are lots of semiprecious gemstones. On many pebble beaches you might find examples of the quartz family of stones. Examples include citrine, jasper, flint, chalcedony, agate, rose quartz, and smoky quartz.

TUMBLE POLISHING

To see the full beauty of these stones they need to be polished or varnished. You can hand polish stones by using emery paper but it is slow and very hard work. The best technique is tumble polishing. This uses a machine that has a rotating drum into which you place the pebbles, a grinding powder, and some water. It can take weeks of polishing to achieve a mirrorlike polish. Once the stones are polished they can be put in settings to make your own jewelry. Tumble polishers are very noisy so you will need an isolated space or understanding neighbors.

Most hobby shops sell beginners' polishing kits, or you could construct a tumble polisher yourself. All you need is a screw-top plastic drum and a slow-running electric motor to turn it.

Tumble polishing can turn dull pebbles from the beach into beautiful, shiny stones.

HOW A DIAMOND IS CUT

Rough diamonds can vary a great deal in shape. They often have to be cleaved (split) before they are shaped (cut) and polished. Diamonds are cut and given faces, called facets, by holding them against a revolving metal plate covered in diamond dust — nothing else is hard enough to cut them! The huge Cullinan diamond was cut into nine large stones and 96 smaller stones.

rough diamond

sawed

rounded

lopped

finished diamond

LITTLE GEMS

All gems, such as diamonds and amethysts, are precious stones made of minerals. They are considered particularly valuable when cut and polished, although many people believe that good examples of the natural crystals are just as beautiful. Usually, it is the beautiful, rare and hard-wearing minerals that have had the greatest value for mounting in jewelry.

A RARE BEAUTY

Gems have been collected and used for thousands of years. Centuries ago, gems were being carved in China, and in Germany there is a tradition of carving cameos that dates back to the Romans. Cameos are produced by cutting away colored layers of material to reveal other layers below.

During the Middle Ages, gemstones were thought to have magical healing properties, a belief that has recently come back into fashion. Jewellers set the gem so that it was in contact with the skin of the wearer. The idea was to allow what were believed to be "health-giving rays" to enter the body.

In astrology, each month has birthstones. Many people believe that wearing your birthstone brings you luck.
1: Garnet (January). 2: Amethyst (February). 3: Aquamarine (above) and bloodstone (below) (March). 4: Diamond (above) and rock crystal (below) (April). 5: Emerald and chrysoprase (May). 6: Moonstone and pearl (June). 7: Ruby and carnelian (July). 8: Peridot and sardonyx (August).
9: Lapis lazuli and sapphire (September).
10: Tourmaline and opal (October).
11: Topaz (November). 12: Zircon and turquoise (December).
The sardonyx (8) is in the form of a cameo.

A QUESTION OF LUCK

Dates of birth have been linked to particular gemstones that are thought to bring good fortune to the wearer. Starting with the birthstone for January, which is garnet, the year then continues with amethyst, bloodstone, diamond, emerald, pearl, ruby, sardonyx, sapphire, opal, topaz, and finishes with turquoise for December.

Some gems are associated with bad luck. The best known is opal. For example, during the European "Black Death" of the Middle Ages, opal was believed to shine when the wearer caught the plague and go dull when the wearer died. Opals have been mined in central Europe for centuries, but many now come from Australia. Although it is quite a hard mineral, opal sometimes cracks if given a hard knock.

Opals (right) have colors that change with the direction of the light shining on them. Opals are often mined by hand (above).

9

11

10

12

A GOOD IMITATION

Since gems are valuable, many attempts have been made to prepare imitation gemstones — sometimes to cheat the buyer. Different types of glass are used and the material is usually called paste or strass. The difficulty is to get the correct combination of hardness, color, and brilliancy in the imitation.

One type of imitation stones uses a real cut gem for the upper part with a paste imitation attached below. These counterfeit gems are called doublets. They are difficult to detect but sometimes the glue loosens when warmed or treated with a solvent. As a result the doublet falls apart.

Sometimes particular colors of natural gems are more valuable. This has encouraged people to change the colors of cheaper stones to make them seem more valuable. Heat or radiation can be used to modify the colors of gems, such as zircon.

These stones are natural brown and heat-treated blue zircon. The paste opal necklace, brooch, and earrings (below) were made in the 18th century.

Once your collection of rocks and fossils has begun to grow, you will need to plan how best to store and display your samples. It is important to be selective when choosing samples to take home, because rocks and fossils take up much more space than stamps, for example. Once you have taken your samples home, you will only be able to display some of them. As your collection grows, choose the best specimens to keep, and store others temporarily in case they can be swapped with other collectors. This is a very good way to extend the range of your own collection.

Large specimens (right) can safely be displayed on shelves. It may be better to store small, light, or fragile samples in trays (below).

STORAGE

For basic storage you will need some trays that can be divided up into compartments. Secondhand furniture may provide you with the basics — filing cabinets or cupboards equipped with shelves are both suitable. The cheapest method is to construct trays yourself using hardboard and strips of wood. Another advantage of home construction is that partitions of different sizes can be made to hold your many different samples.

You can use cardboard boxes or strips of wood or card to separate your specimens in their trays. Divisions improve the look of the collection as well as organize it.

DISPLAY

Illuminated glass shelves are a good way to display the most interesting examples from your collection. Experiment with light shining at different angles to get the best effect from your specimens. Even if you don't have space for glass shelving, you can change your display occasionally, bringing out new specimens just as they do in museums.

As part of your display you can include maps of the area, especially geological maps that show the underlying rock strata. A collection of field sketches and line drawings of fossils or other samples will also prove useful. If you have a special interest, such as in beach sand samples, you may need to develop different display ideas. For example, a collection of stoppered glass containers will be suitable for powders or other small samples.

Museum displays will give you ideas about how to show off your most prized specimens. Include a reference card with each sample so that other people can read the full details.

KEEPING RECORDS

A good system for keeping records is essential, since within a few years your collection may contain hundreds of specimens. To label your samples, paint a small spot of enamel paint onto each of them. When the paint is dry, add a reference number. You can extend the system by color coding, using white for minerals and yellow for fossils, for example.

Write the same reference number on a file card, together with details of the sample. If you have the use of a computer with a spreadsheet, you can keep computer records instead. With a word-processing program the records can be more comprehensive and are easily updated.

Use bright enamel paint to place reference spots and numbers on specimens. Use different colors for the different types. A simple card index will make it easier to keep track of your collection as it grows.

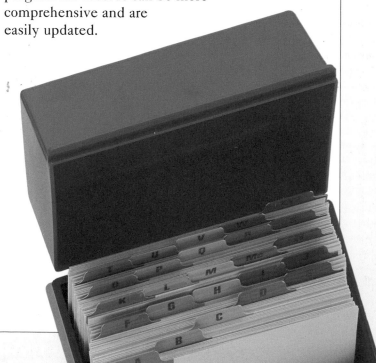

ADVANCING YOUR HOBBY

What next? There are many ways in which rock, mineral, and fossil collectors can develop their hobby. Some choose to specialize in a particular field of study, others enter a career in a related area.

A SPECIALIST COLLECTION

With over 3,000 minerals, plus many types of rocks and fossils, most collectors soon decide to specialize in just one subject. For example, if you live in an area with good fossil deposits you might decide to build a collection of fossils. You can swap specimens with collectors from other areas, or buy from dealers, and you will probably find a section of the local museum or library that has useful references for study. Or you can specialize in the fossils of your local area, becoming an expert on the fossil deposits.

Some experts devote their time to a very specialist subject, seeking gemstones. Most people are familiar with gems such as diamond and sapphire; specialists look for gems that are uncommon in jewelry, or varieties of common gems that have unusual colors.

Collecting stamps that show rocks, fossils, minerals, and dinosaurs can make an interesting sideline to your hobby.

PROJECTS

As well as organizing your main collection, why not start a simple project to do when you can't go collecting specimens? Here are a few ideas.

Build a collection of leaflets and advertisements which have details of caves and other interesting features. If you go on a trip to one of these areas, you'll have some useful background information before you arrive.

A survey of local road names will tell you a great deal about the geology of the surrounding area. Quarry Road and Brickpit Lane are probably common examples; Alum Lane might be a bit more unusual.

If you enjoy photography or drawing, why not make an album of the various rocks used in buildings, or the ways in which fossils have been used in designs for buildings, wallpaper, and fabrics?

Make a survey of buildings, memorials, and gravestones to find the rocks used to make them. Do *not* take samples from any of them! If you can't find the date on a building, look at old photographs or maps to estimate when they were built.

MAKING A CAREER

It's worth thinking about all aspects of your hobby. If your sketches are good, perhaps you could have a career in graphics, specializing in earth science. If you really enjoy communicating your interest to others, you might make a successful teacher, and lead others to study this fascinating subject.

A career as a geologist is an option for someone with a strong interest in the scientific side of the subject. Geologists are employed by many industries and particularly by oil, construction and water companies. For example, if a new bridge or dam is to be constructed, geologists must first check that the local rocks are suitable for building on.

FULL-TIME STUDY

Anyone with a serious interest in becoming a geologist will need to study science at an advanced level. Many schools teach courses in geology and the earth sciences, although most students do not specialize until they enter higher education.

If you want to know more, your school's guidance counselor and companies employing geologists can provide information and advice. One way to find out if you are making a sensible career choice is to arrange work experience with a company.

SOME USEFUL ADDRESSES

Geological Inquiries Group
U.S. Geological Survey, 907 National Center
Reston, VA 22092

Geological Society of America
Educational Programs, P.O. Box 9140
Boulder, CO 80301

American Museum of Natural History
Central Park West at 79th Street
New York, NY 10024

The Field Museum of Natural History
Roosevelt Drive at Lake Shore Drive
Chicago, IL 60605

San Diego Natural History Museum
P.O. Box 1390
San Diego, CA 92112

Many professional scientists and geologists (left) started their careers as a result of collecting rocks and fossils. There are many fascinating careers, such as using laser beams to monitor faults in earthquake zones (below), that use the knowledge and skills you will develop with your hobby.

INDEX